I.AM.RELEVANT

Published by **Relevant Books**
A division of **Relevant Media Group, Inc**.

www.relevant-books.com
www.relevantmediagroup.com

© 2002 by **Relevant Media Group, Inc**.

Design by **Relevant Solutions**
Bobby Jones, Greg Lutze, Daniel Ariza
www.relevant-solutions.com

International Standard Book Number: 0-9714576-0-3

For information:
RELEVANT MEDIA GROUP, INC.
POST OFFICE BOX 951127
LAKE MARY, FL 32795
407-333-7152

Library of Congress Catalog Number: 2002093009

02 03 04 05 9 8 7 6 5 4 3 2
Printed in the United States of America

I.AM.RELEVANT

A GENERATION IMPACTING THEIR WORLD WITH FAITH

FOREWORD BY JARS OF CLAY LEAD SINGER
DAN HASELTINE

CONTENTS

ARTS

MINISTRY

ABOUT THE AUTHORS

FOREWORD

BY.DAN HASELTINE
LEAD SINGER, JARS OF CLAY

I sat in the chair anxious for what was about to take place. I tried not to think about the impending pain. I just stared at the wall adorned with the artistic statements born under the skin of those who came before me. As I took in all of the magnificent designs and intricate sketches, a feeling of inferiority came over me. My design was simple. It was just two Chinese characters. I watched the man in a chair next to me getting some touch-ups to the bikini-clad woman riding the rhino skeleton he had branded across his chest. I began rolling in my mind the host of different reactions I would get from family members, friends, and even strangers. I'm not sure what kept me in the chair. Perhaps it was pride. If I had gotten up, I would have had to face the jibes of friends, and come to grips with the fact I wasn't man enough to go through with it. So, I sat. I waited for nearly 30 minutes. Long enough to really build up in my mind how painful it would be. I created a vision of a giant needle burrowing into my skin. I remembered the torture scene from the movie *Braveheart*. I pictured the tattoo artist standing over me dressed in a burlap robe, telling me if I didn't surrender he would paint a giant turkey vulture across my chest. I thought about screaming "Freedom!"

I handed him the piece of paper upon which I had drawn my simple design of two Chinese characters symbolizing salt and light. I was expecting to be questioned about my choice of design. I knew people had gotten Chinese symbols before, but salt was somewhat unusual. Without a word he began creating the template. I scanned the wall of designs one more time, looked over my shoulder at the nearly finished rhino-skeleton-riding beach blonde, and realized the artists probably stopped inquiring about the designs they were inking a long time ago. He finished the template. We settled on a location just up from the watch line on the inside of my right arm. Highly visible. "Do you want other people to read it or do you want to read it?" I responded, "Other people should not have to read it." He did not quite understand what I meant. He just turned the image around and made the imprint on my arm.

He fired up the bludgeoning device and went to work. I was amazed at his skill, speed, and accuracy as he pushed the needle back and forth around the curvature of the design. He was truly an artist. I was also very relieved to know the pain would be over soon. But I suppose art has never been born without some form of pain attached to it.

To some, tattoo parlors represent the dregs of society, the epitome of our sinful nature along with the porn shops and strip clubs, bars, and psychic reading kiosks. These are places that drip poison into the hearts and minds of those struggling to live a life of pure thought and deed. They are entrees in the buffet of destructive temptations, places where some might conclude darkness has found a way to eclipse light. Many of us have come to believe these are unlikely places to find real beauty, or any redemptive power working.

Upon the walls of Sunset Strip Tattoo Parlor under the fluorescent lights there exists a parable of God's grace and mercy. It finds voice in every painful pierce of a needle and in every birth of an intricate design. It is unearthed in the testimony of skilled craftsmanship and in branded expressions inked across the skin of searching souls. Where there is beauty there is God. Where there is creation there is God. Where there is searching there is God. Where there is God there is passion, fire, and an overwhelming sense that He is good, but not safe. In these places God has made himself known as One who cares little to restrict Himself in His approach to redemption by working only in ways we, His creation, would dub appropriate or possible. God's story has always been placed upon the backdrop of unlikely places. This is true whether we understand it, approve of it, and see it, like it or not.

Because of God's commitment to loving people in wild and unpredictable ways, we His people must carry with us an image of God that is wild with jealousy, undeniably reckless and methodically unpredictable in the approach to pursuing the lost watching world. Have we as image bearers laid claim to these very same characteristics? Have we come to know the God of parting seas, and burning bushes? Have we come to know the God of treacherous storms, and resurrections? He is good. He is not safe.

Within the structure of the modern church a stray belief has developed regarding effective ministry. It is a completely recognizable tattoo on the outer skin of the evangelical community. It presupposes that the qualifying attribute of effective evangelism is a squeaky clean

I.AM.RELEVANT

image. It implies we are good witnesses for Christ only when we have our world in proper perspective, our spiritual life in order, and our suit dry cleaned and pressed. It is this doctrine that cuts at the Achilles heel of true faith. The Gospel has always been about one beggar showing another beggar where to find food. The Gospel of salvation only matters to those who are aware of their need of rescue. I would venture to say that the idea of such perfect imaging was created by people who have long forgotten they too are in constant need of rescue.

God has chosen liars and thieves, lepers, and whores to tell the story of his love. He uses the blind and the deaf, the homeless and the greedy, the selfish and the faithless. He has used evil kings and lowly shepherds. He has used simple-minded children and self-righteous priests. These are the imperfect conduits of God's love and mercy. The people of God's wild redemption tale are an equally unlikely cast. This was true to form in the story of Jonah.

A supply boat set sail from the port of Joppa to Tarshish carrying a few travelers and a small crew. The crewmembers were storing last-minute supplies while the last of the paying travelers climbed aboard. It was a calm morning and the sea was quiet this time of year. A bell rang the final call as a pale, slightly disheveled man ran down the dock and dropped a few coins out of his sweaty hand into the shipmates rusty bucket. He climbed down the plank as his eyes scanned the lively deck. Having noticed there was little activity down below, he climbed down the ladder and took a spot in a dimly lit corner away from the other travelers. Once they were at sea, He would rest. He had been running for a long time. His bones ached like winter, and his head was heavy with the kind of purpose only guilt could birth. He began to feel the gentle rocking of the vessel. His eyes grew heavy and he fell fast asleep. While he slept, a great wind came across the water and swirled the sea and sky into a violent storm. The crewmembers and travelers all began to pray to their gods to be delivered from this angry cloud. It was as if the waves had made a deal with the wind so that they would all be carried to crest upon the boat from any direction. With every futile prayer came more waves, and more wind. The boat was threatening to break apart, so they cried out again, "Who has caused such misfortune to come to us?" They cast lots and found blame in the one man fast asleep below deck. Jonah was awakened by his accusers and brought to the upper deck. "Who are you? What have you done?" they asked. "I am a Hebrew and I worship the Lord, the God of heaven, who made the sea and the land."

To understand the significance of this moment we must first be introduced to the person of Jonah. He was a minister of God who found himself so deep inside the moral law of religion that he could not make a way to love God's plan of grace and forgiveness. He hated the idea that perpetual sinners could receive God's ever-flowing gift of perpetual mercy.

The story of Jonah begins by stating: The word of the Lord came to Jonah, "Go to the great city of Nineveh and preach against it, because its wickedness has come up before me." But Jonah ran away from the Lord and headed for Tarshish. He went down to Joppa and found a ship heading for that port. After paying the fare, he went aboard and sailed for Tarshish to flee the Lord" (Jonah 1:1-3). Jonah hated the city of Nineveh. He hated the people of that great city with a deep-seated passion. He wanted to see them burn in hell. He did not want to preach to them because he knew that meant God would forgive them and show mercy to them. Jonah knew he would have to love these people. He would be the vessel sharing with them living water, salvation for their souls. Jonah wanted absolutely no part of that. So he ran.

A mentor of mine once spoke to me about leadership. He said you can tell a true leader by his reluctance to be in a position of leadership. Be wary of those too comfortable with being in such positions of power. True leaders know what is required of them. They understand that the model of leadership Jesus Christ set up for us was one of servitude. They know that leadership is far less about visible strength than it is about transparent weakness. To be a leader the will must be crushed. The resistance to die to our own purpose that continues to grow must be reckoned with on a continual basis. Jonah was an example of a man who knew what was required of him.

But God gave Jonah a gift. Just before Jonah is thrown into the sea and swallowed by a giant fish, God showed Jonah how far He would go to reach the lost. God opens Jonah's eyes to how wild and unpredictable His schemes can become. By using such blatant rebellion along with Jonah's own testimony about the God he served, He brought salvation to the wandering sailors caught in Jonah's storm.

For my tattoo, I chose Chinese symbols to remind me of the God I met among the people of the underground church in China—a magical, aggressive, merciful God who could bring such vivid joy in the midst of suffering and laughter in the presence of injustice and true freedom in the clutches of political slavery. Salt reminds me that through Christ I have the power and the great pleasure of seasoning life with passion. And light is the only thing people search for in the dark places of the world.

We, the Body of Christ, have all faced the stifling opinion of order. Age-old traditions have chipped away at us, and we have come to believe something as wild as love could be contained in patterns and rituals. We have come to believe something as intoxicating and explosive as saving grace could be bound and gagged like a hostage to only our altar calls and rededication ceremonies.

The church has lost its power to love because we have rendered the God of love powerless by covering the only truth that speaks to the depths of the heart and soul in a shroud of pious doctrine, false-righteousness, religious politics, and moral policing. We have gotten so exclusive in our insular Christian lifestyle we have given real people with real issues no alternative but to deem the Gospel irrelevant or inconsequential.

There is a sense of hopelessness about the modern church in America. A feeling that those who came before have set an irreversible perception in place by which the world will perpetuate its angry biases. If you share in this despair I pray that this book will encourage you. The church is very much a main character in the story of salvation and redemption.

We are standing at a point in history. A line has been drawn in the sand. It is now the time to reclaim the real attributes of Christ. We have seen the great divide created in our culture between the body of Christ and the watching world. It is our turn to build bridges and believe in a love that drives out fear, a love that seeks not to convert, not to fill church buildings, not to make people think like we do, but simply to love as far as God will reach. We need to give up the "us against them" mentality. Let us assume the posture of a beggar showing another beggar where to find food. We must attempt to fulfill real needs, and have faith God will call His own to Himself. For the labyrinth of the heart is severely complex, and the wounds run deep. God alone can bind up the broken hearted. We must simply seek to serve. Our honesty, transparency, and love are what drive us to true relevance in a cynical, jaded post-Christian culture.

Within the pages of this book are stories of God's people. They are stories of reluctant leaders and long distance runners. Like Jonah they have been given the gift of seeing just how far God's redeeming love will reach. They know it has no end, and His thirst for loving will never be quenched. The people in these pages share a common vision. They still look for God in the dark places. They still seek to believe in a God of love who with wild abandon uses the whole of creation to serve the purpose of redemption. They are stripping away the negative effects of bad religious practices to reveal a Gospel of substance and truth, timeless in its ability to shed light and life in a decaying world. They are people very much aware of their desire to run away from God, and more aware of God's relentless pursuit of them. They serve because they have been served. They love because they have been loved. Who are these people, you ask? They are relevant.

INTRODUCTION

BY.CAMERON STRANG
PRESIDENT/CEO,
RELEVANT MEDIA GROUP

At a massive Christian retail industry trade show, two men stood outside the convention center holding large white signs that said "PRAY FOR REVIVAL!" in bold black letters. Every day, the men tirelessly stood on the sidewalk across the street, waving their signs and motioning at every pedestrian and car that passed by.

As I crossed the street near them one afternoon on my way to lunch, they spotted me and yelled, "Pray for revival, brother!" I sheepishly smiled, nodded, then avoided eye contact and picked up the pace in my walk. As I passed by, they suddenly turned to me and again yelled, "Pray for revival, BROTHER!" About scared me to death.

A few days later, a friend of mine attended a Major League baseball game in the same city. During the seventh inning stretch, he saw one of those same men appear, but this time he was running across the outfield frantically waving a "JESUS LOVES YOU" sign in front of 30,000 fans. Security chased him down, tackled him, and dragged him off the field kicking and fighting. As my friend told me the story, I shook my head in disbelief. What could have been going through that man's mind? How could he be so out of touch?

Not two days after the baseball game, that same friend and I were attending a basketball All-Star Game in another state. As we settled into our seats, hot dogs and sodas in-hand, the unthinkable happened. We saw him.

The same guy from the convention. The one who yelled at me. The one who got arrested at the baseball game. Somehow, he had gotten down on the floor of the arena, and sure enough, he casually held a large "JESUS LOVES YOU" sign by his side. He wandered around for a few minutes and found an empty seat behind the basket. As the game started, he held the sign up. Security promptly came and asked him to put it away. He complied. But my friend and I knew he was really there to run.

About four minutes into the first period, there was a foul. As the teams walked to the opposite end of the court for the ensuing free throws, he crouched. With a shiver of excitement, we knew this was it. In one swift motion, the man lunged out of his seat with his sign fully raised and his feet scampering. He bee-lined it for center court, where he waved the sign around until a security guard ran out and ushered him off. We were so disappointed! If only the security guard had left him alone, I'm sure he would have shared the Gospel, given an altar call, and 17,000 lives would have been forever changed. We could have seen a great revival happen in that basketball arena that night.

The whole episode, though somewhat surreal, reminds me of the street evangelists who hang out downtown in our city. With megaphones blazing, every weekend they wave signs and tell everyone within earshot they're going to hell if they don't repent. I've never seen these street evangelists actually engage someone in conversation—they just seem to take truth and stab with it. They stand there yelling hellfire and brimstone and come across as crazy. Why would a non-Christian want to listen to their message? *If this is a life sold out to Jesus*, they think, *count me out*.

For the life of me, I can't find a passage in the Bible where Jesus broke the law by running out on the field during sporting events, waving stupid signs to tell the crowd He loves them. I don't recall Him kicking and fighting when security guards tackled him. I don't even read where He screamed at people on the side of the road to pray for revival. The Jesus I know engaged the lives of people around Him. He boldly spoke truth in love. He dined with sinners and formed relationships with them. He won them through His grace, through His forgiveness and mercy. He shared truth, and it drew people. He confronted Pharisees, but embraced sinners.

As a Christian, I was embarrassed at that All-Star game. No wonder mainstream society treats believers as second-class citizens. It's not because of our faith—it's because the only Christians they see yell in megaphones, ask for money on TV, or bomb abortion clinics.

It's basic marketing, people. Christians have the best product ever invented—hope, eternal life, and salvation from hell through Christ. It should be the easiest sales pitch ever. There must be a reason Ford employees don't stand on sidewalks screaming at people for not driving Fords. Marketing 101 teaches that you don't want your audience put off by you. You want them to trust you and trust your message. You're not trying to push something down their throats; you're simply letting them know about something they actually want. By getting to know your audience and being sensitive to your environment, you'll be more able to more effectively reach those around you and enact change.

Isn't it time for the Church, the largest and best "corporation" in the world, to start investing a little more thought into its marketing strategy? We have the very thing that everyone on the planet is looking for, whether they know it or not. It's just a matter of effectively reaching them with our message and being more relevant in our approach.

How did Jesus do it? How is He calling you to do it? That's the central message of this book. By examining the lives of seventy other people just like you, we're showing a variety of ways people are effectively fulfilling the Great Commission today. Maybe you'll identify with a story in here. Maybe you'll be inspired to step out and make your own.

Our job as followers of Christ is to love Him, and reflect that love to those around us. That doesn't mean we have to stand on a street corner, wave signs, and scream. It means we need to live out our faith twenty-four hours a day, seven days a week. It means we need to get outside our comfort zones and make a difference in the real world. The individuals collected in this book are doing just that. They're part of a groundswell movement that's sparking change in our generation and culture. These aren't the old leaders toiling only in the churches, completely unaware of what's happening in the world around them. They're out there where Jesus was: With people. Touching lives. Changing things.

The people in this book have taken risks. They've sacrificed. They've stood alone. But they're living out their faith in a very relevant way, and they're making a mark on eternity. As you flip through the pages of this book, notice how they're touching lives. Some are overt, some are subtle. All are effective. These people live in the same world you do. They just decided to take their faith and do something about it. Will you?

I.AM.RELEVANT

CULTURE
SECTION.ONE

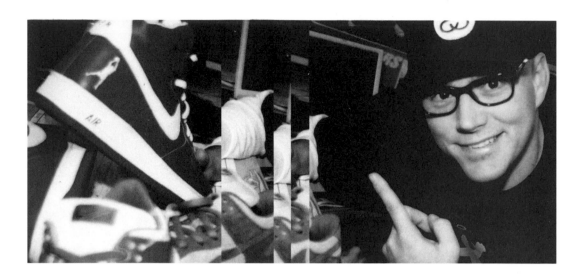

ROBBIE JEFFERS

AGE:32
BIRTHPLACE:CARSON, CALIFORNIA
OCCUPATION:SALES/MARKETING FOR STUSSY, NIKE

Sometimes the most incredible events in life aren't front-page stories. Robbie Jeffers' wonder years as a "chillin' white middle class kid from Huntington Beach" don't score as a made-for-TV drama, and at fifteen, his painless conversion to Christianity at an Altar Boys concert doesn't blow as a mind-numbing testimony. These days, his job entails managing and directing professional skateboarders, wallowing in free gear, and caring for his wife and two-year-old daughter, Selah.

However, Jeffers' Orange County life digs much deeper. "I'm known in the industry as that Christian team manager or that Christian guy at Stussy," he says. Proud of the association but all too aware of its momentous responsibility, he says, "A lot of big skaters ask me for advice sometimes. God uses my position to reach a lot of these high-profile skaters and lead by example. I'm the only Bible these guys will ever read." He pauses a moment. "I know they watch."

His phone rings again. Throughout the interview, Jeffers' phone has been ringing like Miss Cleo's, and as I gaze around the room, I'm in style wonderland. Rasheed Wallace Nikes (one of five pairs made), Mark Gonzales art, wall-to-wall shoes and skateboard decks. How did this guy get here?

In true American dream tradition, he started as a janitor. "I started out sweeping the warehouse here," he relates without hesitation. He advanced in his job, and when the skateboarding and urban clothing market began to reconfigure, Stussy's owner approached him to man the wheel of their skate department.

"I basically put a face to Stussy's name," Jeffers says. Not the easiest task when you're talking about a twenty-year-old company that took the surf/skate world by storm, transformed youth fashion in America and the world over, and is still alive and kicking. But after he directed the corporation back into the open arms of the skate industry, some company named Nike gave Robbie a holler.

"Nike has always been a big admirer of Stussy, saw how Stussy got into skateboarding and as far as presence in Japan; they appreciated what I had done and they asked me to do the same for them," he explains.

So what exactly is Jeffers doing? "Just trying to invent new looks while keeping in touch with who we are," he says. "Basically, Nike's a $9 billion major corporation that I'm trying to take underground, and I'm accomplishing that with the riders I picked up. I didn't go after the superstars, I went after the 'skater' skater—riders who were respected amongst their peers. Not the flavor-of-the-month skater, but someone with longevity."

That doesn't mean he hasn't attracted the attention of big-namers. The A-list of the industry has been riding him like a merry-go-round to get sponsored, yet Jeffers' heart shows through as he remarks, "I didn't do anything; I don't have any accomplishments; I'm just being truthful. Other people might see otherwise, but I think God just orchestrated it all and used Balaam's donkey here."—*Bobby Kim*

I.AM.RELEVANT

STEPHANIE RICHARDS

AGE:24
BIRTHPLACE:ORLANDO, FLORIDA
OCCUPATION:MODEL, PAINTER

For Stephanie Richards, painting was something she just had to do. It flowed out of her as naturally as speech. As a teen, she decided to pursue it further by attending art school. She dreamed of living in Paris someday, painting professionally around the world. However, barely existing as an art student of modest means made that seem impossible.

Toward the beginning of her art school career, an Italian photographer and a Los Angeles modeling agency approached Richards about modeling. Even though she initially turned them down, before she knew it she was doing a shoot for the cover of a magazine. Within months she was asked to pursue a modeling career, at the expense of art school.

Soon, Richards was in the middle of a movie plot—a small town kid thrown in over her head into a business with a frequently dark side. She was immediately jetting off to cities all over the world. She was alone and in various strange places. The industry itself was cutthroat and friends were hard to find. It's easy to imagine what emotions followed: loneliness, despair, hopelessness. The more she moved up in the modeling world, the more miserable and empty she felt.

It was during this time Richards found solace in the museums and old cathedrals of Europe. Even though she felt depressed and guilty, she could find God present in the beauty of those surroundings. She would skip fashion castings to roam through the art museums, walk the streets where Picasso lived, and paint the canals of Venice—just as she had dreamed of doing while in art school.

While back in the States, Richards heard an evangelist. "His words pierced my heart," she says. "I saw people my age deeply in love with Jesus. I knew they had something I had lost. I felt I had gone too far and that Christ would not accept me back. One afternoon while visiting the MET in New York City, I broke down in tears. I decided to find a church and get right with God. I went to David Wilkerson's Times Square Church. I stood in the back, eyes filled with tears, and my heart broken before God."

Within a year, she had begun a Bible study and Christian group within the fashion industry. She watched in amazement as God changed and filled the lives of famous models, photographers, and agents.

About half a year ago, Richards received a traumatic brain injury in a near-fatal car accident. For a time, she could not even sign her name. Painting was out of the question, and it seemed like the chance of creating works of beauty would never happen again. However, she has recovered: "With the Lord's help, determination, and therapy I've done nearly a full turn-around," she says. "I'm even creating works I am very proud of." It also seems that with Richards' life, God is making a work He can be proud of.—*Daniel Miller*

THOMAS HORRELL

AGE:24
BIRTHPLACE:NASHVILLE, TENNESSEE
OCCUPATION:WAKESKATE ENTREPRENEUR

Thomas Horrell does his own thing. At twenty-four, the Florida resident has already gone pro, invented his own sport, and started his own company.

Growing up in Winter Haven, Florida, Horrell knew several people who wakeboarded and picked up the sport at the age of fourteen. He went pro around the age of seventeen, but by the time he was twenty-one he'd decided that it was time for a change. Instead of changing sports, though, he decided to invent his own.

Skateboarding was his first love, so Horrell began looking for a way to combine his two favorite sports. He and his friends designed their own wakeskate boards (instead of the foam, fiberglass, and binding that are characteristic of a wakeboard, the board functions more like a skateboard, made of wood and using grip tape) by cutting down their old wakeboards. A year later, he and his friends started their own company, Cassette Wakeskate. Horrell has been wakeskating for the past three years, and has a number of sponsors; he gets a boat, sunglasses, backpacks, energy drinks, and the like for free.

They say imitation is the highest form of flattery, so Horrell should be proud. Several companies are now designing boards like his. But despite Horrell's innovation, his ideas are provoking criticism from an industry that is mostly focused on waterskiing. "I try to do things differently, so I've been criticized," Horrell says. "I have ideas that people aren't familiar with, so it does come off kinda weird because I'm trying to introduce some other ideas that they haven't thought of."

Horrell moved to Orlando four years ago, and spends the majority of his time either wakeskating or working with Cassette, making and selling boards, working with wakeskate artists, spending time on videos and the magazine, and trying to grow the company. His Christian faith, which he's had since childhood, has been obvious to his coworkers. "I've never been one to shout orders to people in regard to religion," Horrell says. "But the people who know me know that I treat people right and I'm a Christian ... people see that and know that's what I'm into."

Horrell's goals for the immediate future are simple: "To sell some more boards and make more money," he says. "And to make the company as good as it can be." As for personal goals, "finding a nice girl" is on the top of his list, although he's not crying himself to sleep over it every night. "When I'm ready to get married God will tell me, but I'm not too worried about it right now," Horrell concedes. "I'm too busy anyway."—*Maria Southman*

I.AM.RELEVANT

CHADWICK AND HOLLY PELLETIER

AGES:CHADWICK 28; HOLLY 22
BIRTHPLACES:CHADWICK: DENVER, COLORADO; HOLLY: MEADOW VISTA, CALIFORNIA
OCCUPATIONS:CHADWICK: ACTOR, WRITER, MARTIAL ARTIST, MEDICAL PROFESSIONAL; HOLLY: PROPERTY MANAGER

How ironic is it that "reality television" is differentiated as its own television genre, riding on the faulty notion that unlike other TV programs, it's unbound by inclement editing, set storylines, and sensationalist angles. Unfortunately, the "reality" remains that as long as there's a top-dog telling the story and calling the shots, reality and television will forever remain estranged bed buddies.

No one is as down to testify for this hard truth than Chadwick and Holly Pelletier, past stars of *Road Rules*—MTV's *Real World* spin-off documenting "real" people (oftentimes strikingly attractive with marketable vices) forced to live/bicker with each other in a Winnebago. The newlyweds were recently invited back to the small screen as the infamous married couple on *Real World/Road Rules Challenge: Battle of the Seasons,* but the show didn't necessarily go according to plan for the Pelletiers, especially considering the editors' resolution to shape the two as evil personified.

Chadwick, a Harvard grad, Martial Arts Hall-of-Famer, and regarded downhill skier, confides, "I thought [this show] was really about reputation repair from the first show. After seeing the editing, I was thinking, 'You've got to be kidding me. I'm not that person, I didn't do that; I'm talking about somebody else.' They could have literally made me fall in love with another guy on that show if they wanted to. The editors are genius."

Holly adds, "It's frustrating having to play their game, but I'm also grateful for the experiences and the chances I've been given to speak."

Grateful for being sliced and diced on national television? Chadwick explains, "I realized it was never about me or Holly; it was about God. You watch the show now, this is amazing—Holly's praying and they're keeping our shirts that say 'Jesus Christ' on there. The response from that, it's been all worth it."

Holly agrees. "If you can get MTV to show people praying, then God is *big*! It's huge!" she says. "It's an experience not many people get to have, let alone have when you're in the grace of God, doing the right thing ... it was a blessing. It's an exposure I've been given and if I waste it, it's a crime. I've been given a chance to use a voice, and if I don't use it the way it should be used, then I'm in the wrong."

Using that voice to represent God isn't always a cakewalk, as Chadwick recounts: "One of my clients' bosses told her, 'I can't believe you're training with Chadwick; he's the biggest jerk!' After the first show, I'd get hate mail, jail mail, stuff I don't even want to tell you. It just became so tedious, so tiring, that I just gave it to God. I said, 'I don't know why I was on the show to begin with...'" He collects his thoughts and says, "But I think it's coming full circle."
—*Bobby Kim*

I.AM.RELEVANT

MATT
DEGEN

AGE:26
BIRTHPLACE:DOWNEY, CALIFORNIA
OCCUPATION:JOURNALIST

The corporate newsroom—a place of cynicism and skepticism. Throw it smack into Southern California, a land of silicone and sensationalism, and you have a ripe mission field for living out a vibrant faith in approachable and positive garments.

Matt Degen is venturing along such a terrain, spending nights as a copy editor, concert reviewer, and pop music critic—particularly, Christian pop—for the heavily-circulated *Orange County Register*. It isn't the place he expected to be or even the vocational niche he longed for, but Degen has a clear sense of God's call as he strolls into the editorial offices and feels the pulse and hum.

Upon graduating from Cal State-Fullerton, Degen hoped to land a "dream job" in advertising. Doors were rusted shut, so he parlayed some college copy editing experience into a position as a news assistant at the *Register*. "I was the lowest man on the totem pole, but I loved the energy of working at a newspaper," Degen says. "The Lord showed me that's where I need to be. I felt this incredible sense of belonging there."

Others noticed his hard work, and Degen was given the chance to write some music reviews. This led to him being granted an existing column on Christian music called "Higher Ground," which allows him a lot of creative control. Another hat he wears is as a video game editor. "It's pretty much my dream job," he says. "I get to listen to music, play video games, and read the paper for a living."

Degen has other pursuits. He recently completed a manuscript that offers "a lighter look from a waiter's point of view of what goes on in a restaurant," based upon a job he held several years ago, and is currently writing a screenplay.

The twenty-six year old was given a strong foundation of faith by his family and has been active in church all of his life. Each night in the newsroom, he encounters an atmosphere much different than your average evangelical church surroundings. "There is a lot of cynicism," he says. "That's kind of what we're taught as reporters and editors in general: If your mother says she loves you, check it out. I think journalists tend to be kind of skeptical creatures to begin with. I think many of them are wary of religion." He adds, "It's cool being able to work with my fellow journalists and say, 'Hey guys, I'm a Christian, but I'm not some wacko, some stereotypical version of whatever you're thinking a Christian is.'"

Degen enjoys the freedom of expressing himself through his Christian music column. "My aim has never been to bash anyone over the head with the Bible. I believe in the real gentle approach. Let people know it's out there, and encourage some exploration."
—*John M. De Marco*

GAVIN
PEACOCK

AGE:34
BIRTHPLACE:LONDON, ENGLAND
OCCUPATION:PROFESSIONAL SOCCER PLAYER

Gavin Peacock was born with a soccer ball at his feet. With a father who played professionally, Gavin grew up on the field, rain or shine, watching his dad play more than five hun-
dred games for Charlton Althletic, the UK team that Gavin joined years later. "Football is in
my blood," he says. "Even my wedding had to be fitted into football!"

Known for scoring vital match-winning goals from his position in mid-field, Peacock, now
thirty-four, has played professional "football" for more than fifteen years in England. And
through advancement and set-back, a loyal fanbase has continued to cheer him on.

In 1993, Peacock's career escalated when he was transferred for more than £1 million to Chelsea, a division one team that witnessed him score fourteen goals his first season. So many, Chelsea even reached the Cup Final that year, which they hadn't done in almost three decades. And it was thanks largely to their new mid-fielder: Peacock scored the only goal in the quarter-final and both goals in the semi-final games.

But when the team went through administrative changes in 1996 and three overseas players were signed on, suddenly Peacock found there was no place for him on the team. "That is the thing about football," he says. "You've got to keep a level head. If you do get carried away, football throws you from one extreme to the other."

During the most tumultuous times, Peacock was able to keep that level head by reminding himself that his life was in Someone else's hands. "He in control. No matter what happens, I think God does carry us through lean periods, through injury periods, but it is only when we look back that we learn in that respect."

When his game was swept out from under him, Peacock was also reminded that true value is in God's eyes, not his coaches' or the media's. "God is the one who gives me my self-worth," he says. "First, I'm a Christian and then second, I am a footballer."

To this day, Peacock is thankful that his "mum" introduced him to Christianity. "When she started going to church I went along a few times to see what it was all about," he says. "I had always believed in God, that He was up there somewhere, but there was never anything personal about it." Eventually, Peacock discovered just how personal a relationship with Christ could be, and he offered his life to Him in full faith.

Now, Gavin sees soccer and faith as inseparable. Even though it's challenging to be civil in a rough and rowdy sport, Gavin tries to keep his ethics both on and off the field. He and his wife Amanda even lead a footballers Bible study in London where fellow soccer players meet to worship, pray, and support each other. —*Jennifer Ashley*

LANCE WILDER

AGE:33
BIRTHPLACE:LOWELL, MASSACHUSETTS
OCCUPATION:ANIMATION DESIGNER

If you've spent any time checking out *The Simpsons* during the past twelve years, you've seen the work of Lance Wilder. No, Wilder isn't really the voice of Krusty the Clown, nor is he the secret persona of misfit ten-year-old Bart or—Dohh!!!—Homer. Look beyond the members of prime time animation's favorite dysfunctional family to the backdrop of Springfield and its surroundings, and you'll see Wilder's efforts as background design supervisor for the long-running series.

The gig with *The Simpsons*, Wilder's first and only job since graduating from the Rhode Island School of Design in 1990, is literally an ongoing dream opportunity. Growing up in Massachusetts, Wilder loved art and its numerous dimensions such as perspective, composition, and hand-eye coordination, and fine-tuned his skills as a college student. A friend turned him on to *The Simpsons* just as the show was beginning to carve out a small cult following, and before graduation the inspiration hit to call the show and ask for a job. "I prayed, 'Just open up a door for me and put it in my heart that I would know exactly where, when, and what I was supposed to do,'" Wilder recalls. "I really felt in my heart *The Simpsons* was it."

Two days after graduation, Wilder was on the set. That summer of 1990, *The Simpsons* became a

I.AM.RELEVANT

huge sensation, with the young and old alike reciting its popular catch phrases. Wilder immersed himself in the fun of working on a hit TV show, hung out with his colleagues, and further refined his craft as he helped design scenery. Gradually, some emptiness set in. Wilder had attended church growing up, but in his new surroundings he was unaware of what church to go to and "didn't know if there was a Christian anywhere in Hollywood." One night, Wilder accidentally stumbled across a Christian radio station. He kept tuning in, taking advantage of the regular use of Walkman radios at work to fill his mind and heart with biblical teachings.

At work, Wilder found himself often rebutting anti-religious or anti-Christian comments made by co-workers. This inspired him to further study Scripture and have good reasons for his beliefs. "My job is to grow and to try to have an answer and set a good example and not be antagonistic or argumentative. To really listen to people where they're coming from and their perspective, and not push anything on them."

After five or six years on the show, Wilder and a few others started a Bible study that has grown to close to fifteen people. Some colleagues bring up spiritual issues and ask for his perspective. Several people have come to Christ during the last two or three seasons at work. "They go to church, read their Bibles, have stopped cussing. They've changed," Wilder says. Maybe there's hope for Bart after all.—*John M. De Marco*

EMANUEL SMITH

AGE:26
BIRTHPLACE:JACKSON, MISSISSIPPI
OCCUPATION:PROFESSIONAL FOOTBALL PLAYER

Emanuel Smith's journey, when viewed under the world's lens of success, has been an undulating one. A star athlete while in high school in Mississippi and part of a middle-class family of six, he played football and basketball, and ran track. He earned a scholarship to the University of Arkansas and chose to concentrate on football—and his long-time dream of playing professionally was rapidly becoming much more than a distant possibility.

Then came some unexpected roadblocks: a torn quad muscle and broken ankle freshman year meant the year of competition was lost, and the subsequent rehabilitation meant that sophomore year was spent just getting back up to speed. His grandmother also passed away, with Smith not getting the chance to see her before she died. "It seemed that the two most important things in my life were taken away from me," he recalls.

Even with a successful last two years playing college football, Smith felt he had little chance of being drafted and concentrated on graduating. He started going to church. "One Sunday I decided that I wanted to change the way I lived," he says. "I invited Jesus into my heart … I knew that having God as the head of my life, everything would be okay. I never looked back after my life changed that day."

With his newfound faith, Smith decided to again pursue his dream of playing professional football. He began to work out again, to get ready for the NFL scouts' day. Even though he was not a featured player on that day, he knew that if he worked to the extent of his ability, God would take care of the rest.

During workouts, he stood out. He was the fastest in the 40. He did well in the drills. He received several invitations from teams to come and do individual workouts. In the end, Smith was drafted in the sixth round by the Jacksonville Jaguars. He graduated from Arkansas with a B.A. in criminal justice. He married and began a life in Florida, where he quickly got involved with Spoken Word Ministries in Jacksonville. He hopes his life and faith reach out to the other players on the Jaguars. "I just want to play football as long as God wants me to," he says. "I know I am in this profession for a reason … I just want to touch the lives of people, mainly young children, and help them to know God."

In the future, Smith knows it will not be the praise of the public, but the direction of God that will guide him through the roads of life. Whether they are smooth or not will be of little consequence to a person who keeps his eyes so firmly fixed.—*Daniel Miller*

CAROLINE LALIVE

AGE:22
BIRTHPLACE:TRUKEE, CALIFORNIA
OCCUPATION:ALPINE SKI RACER

Caroline Lalive describes being a Christian on the United States Ski Team in one word: "lonely." The two-time Olympic racer and only female in America to score World Cup points in all five alpine racing disciplines during the same season says there isn't much fellowship on the racing circuit. "I find I am having to really draw on the Word and seek the Lord for my daily spiritual food," she says. "I find that my prayer life is so important. I am learning the importance of being bold. God is continually giving me opportunities and I [need to] grab hold of them."

Though she has been skiing since she was two years old, Lalive first dreamed of winning an Olympic medal while watching the '88 Calgary Olympics. "I remember watching one of my skiing heroes and he had just won the gold," she recalls. "He was giving an interview and after watching that I went into my room and pretended to give an interview of my own. I even pretended to have the Swiss accent!"

She became part of the Olympic Team in 1995 and began finishing in the top seed, establishing her niche among the best female skiers in the world. "It was a huge mental hurdle for me," she says. "I have had some major spiritual breakthroughs as well. Funny enough, they usually seem to come when I am struggling in my skiing."

By the winter of 2002, she was ranked as high as second in the world in the combined event and fourth in the world in the Super-G. Lalive went into the 2002 Olympic Games as one of the most watched and feared female athletes. NBC even pre-named her "America's Sweetheart" as she was favored to win the difficult combined race (combining two slalom runs and one downhill) on Valentine's Day.

However, Lalive fell three times. Immediately following her Olympic disappointment, fan mail flooded in, prayers and support surrounded her and Lalive went on to win the prestigious silver medal in the Downhill World Cup finals, becoming America's best speed skier. As if that wasn't enough, Lalive finished the season as National Champion with two gold medals in the Combined and Super-G and two silver medals in Slalom and G-S.

Lalive says the results of a race are just a "by-product" or "bonus" for doing what she loves. "The love I have is for the simple elements of skiing and racing," she says. "The sheer joy I get from that nervous feeling standing in the start. The incredible sensation of my skis arcing on the cold smooth snow, with the wind in my face. Where else can you go 80 mph on wooden sticks and everything around flies by at a slower pace because you are in the zone? There will be a day when I will miss those butterflies in my stomach."
—*Margaret Feinberg*

I.AM.RELEVANT

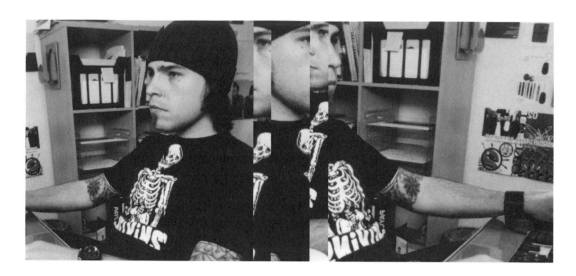

DON
CLARK

AGE:26
BIRTHPLACE:SAN JOSE, CALIFORNIA
OCCUPATION:GRAPHIC DESIGNER

Pursuing a vocational dream can look grim when the economy's in the tank. Especially for techies. Especially if you're young and lacking a descriptive track record. Especially in unemployment mecca Seattle.

Don Clark bought a Mac when they first came out in the early eighties. Attending high school in California, he envisioned one day owning and operating a design studio in Seattle. But a few years back, he was doing something far different and far away.

Clark was a courier for a major shipping company while he and his wife Erika were living in Sacramento. "We were struggling to make ends meet, like most young couples," Clark says. "I had a friend who was a designer up here (in Seattle), and got a job as an art designer at his dot.com."

Clark and Erika prayed about the decision. The timing felt right. Clark had never landed a full-time graphic design job, his longtime dream. They made the move, and for six months it was awesome. He worked alongside his friend Demetri Arges, whom he'd grown up with in California, sharing a mutual love of graphics and music.

"But we got laid off a couple of days before Thanksgiving," Clark continues, "and that was tough, living in a brand new city where the rent's high. But the Lord opened up a door to an even better job, where Demetri and I were able to become art directors at a wireless company for a lot more money. That was about two weeks later."

In July 2001, less than a year after that, another layoff knocked Clark and Arges to the sidelines. But Clark says, "Things have happened the way they should."

What happened was the explosion of a graphic design business, Asterik Studios, that Clark and Arges launched on their own while still employed by the techie firms. They began designing T-shirts and other items for Seattle-based alternative Christian label Tooth and Nail. They've done art for the likes of Starflyer 59, Poor Old Lu, The Blamed, The Dingees, Dead Poetic, Ghoti Hook, Element 101 and numerous other groups that move about the country hanging out with the youth culture and offering positive outlooks on life's choices. Check out www.paparoach.com and stuff from Roadrunner Records (owned by Island F-Jam and the home to Nickelback), and you'll see more of Asterik's handiwork.

"It's kind of grown into something I never thought," says Clark, who once had a record deal with Tooth and Nail himself. "I've done countless interviews with graphic design students at colleges, which is kind of cool because I didn't actually get a degree of my own."

The Asterik guys have also worked for some of Seattle's high-end modern furniture companies, and have gotten into some other corporate/big business design work. "That's where the money is a lot of the time," Clark says, then adds, "The entertainment industry doesn't pay a whole lot, but our love and our passion is the music industry."
—John M. De Marco

I.AM.RELEVANT

STEPHANIE LANIER

AGE: 26
BIRTHPLACE: COMMACK, NEW YORK
OCCUPATION: EXECUTIVE ASSISTANT, MTV

MTV. The home of *Cribs*. Orbiter of *The Real World*. The network that used to get you *Undressed*. And the stomping grounds of a twenty-five-year-old bundle of Long Island energy named Stephanie Lanier, who is making Christ approachable in an environment not known for their moral absolutes.

Lanier hops the LIRR train and a Manhattan-bound subway car each morning, dc Talk blasting in her CD Walkman, a copy of the latest installment of *Left Behind* in her purse. Soon the music will be pouring out from her desktop speakers, and the book will rest conspicuously on the desk of her office at Broadway and 44th Street, where she is executive assistant to the vice president of special events at MTV Networks, center of the pop culture universe.

It's an interesting place to be for someone whose parents never allowed cable in the house when she was growing up—mainly because of the presence of, yes, MTV. But Lanier developed a passion for music after babysitting for Liberty DeVitto's daughters (he's Billy Joel's drummer). After a semester studying broadcast communications at Virginia's Liberty University and returning to Long Island to earn an associate's degree in business, Lanier landed a job at a law firm.

I.AM.RELEVANT

After six months of legalese, Lanier saw an ad for an administrative assistant position at the network's Long Island office. She landed the job, and a year later transferred to MTV headquarters. "I had no encouragement along the way," Lanier says. "When I told people, especially my parents, they would say, 'You don't want to work for them; it's evil.'"

But Lanier's determination to allow her light to shine in the darkness would not be dissolved. And time has confirmed her special calling to MTV. Her special events office includes twelve employees, none of whom aside from Lanier attend church. Among the group are five gay men, including two that are "married" to each other. Lanier is wise and compassionate enough to not allow any particular theological qualms to get in the way of fostering real and relevant relationships, the aspect of our calling that Jesus demonstrated as the most vital.

Lanier's credibility with her colleagues has paid off. During early 2001, an unmarried female co-worker became pregnant. Leaning toward having an abortion, she approached Lanier, unsure if that was the right decision. Lanier gently encouraged her friend to continue with the pregnancy. "In October, she had a baby boy," Lanier happily reports.

Despite the opportunities for such powerful ministry, life as the lone believer at her office—and living as a Christian in New York in general—can be quite discouraging. Bombarded daily with expressions and assertions that don't gel with her biblical values, Lanier has learned to "roll [her] eyes and sort of grin and bear it."

"My philosophy of life is just to be a light, to make a difference within this whole entertainment business," she says. "I'm just trying to be real." —*John M. De Marco*

JOSEPH HENRY KRAFT

AGE:22
BIRTHPLACE:POWAY, CALIFORNIA
OCCUPATION:BIBLE STUDENT, TEACHER, STYLIST

When you're in kindergarten, everybody wants to do the same things when they grow up. Astronaut. Fireman. Doctor. Message-based fashion designer. For Joe Kraft, founder of Volition and Invisible God clothing, the options are limitless.

In fact, he's not only tasted sweet success from following his passions, but he's also making it possible for others to follow in his footsteps. The Retail Project, which will open this year at a regional teen center in San Diego, will operate as a clothing store/school that will "introduce kids to the rag industry at an early age and show them that they don't have to be an engineer if they don't want to," Kraft says. Not only will the store be run and managed by youth, but prominent artists including Obey's Shepard Fairey and Alphanumeric's Alyasha Owerka-Moore will offer insight on the art/fashion industry.

Kraft was initially introduced to the social workings of fashion in the eighth grade, when his brother schooled him on the power of clothing. Within little time, Kraft found a love for sewing and fashion through making T-shirts for his childhood break dancing crew.

From his office in Mira Mesa, he says, "I've always liked how a musician [can] write an album and people will listen to the lyrics because they like the artist and the style, and they'll follow whatever that guy has to say. God hasn't given me the talents in music, so I had to find another way to express myself, and that's through clothing.

"It's like an easy ice-breaker when someone sees your shirt and asks you a question about it, it's an alley-oop to share your faith with them in an aesthetically pleasing way."

Not only does Kraft express himself, but he's also rethinking postmodern fashion through his clothing lines, Volition and Invisible God. "With Volition," Kraft explains, "I'm trying to spread the message of exercising free will to the urban/boardsports lifestyle market. When it all comes down to it with free will, the main choice is deciding whether to serve God or not. And if you choose to use that free will for God, you have power over sin and that's a whole other lifestyle as a Christian."

In terms of Invisible God, Kraft has a separate, yet not entirely different, ideology. "I want to keep it more in boutique stores, high urban fashion ... reaching out to the rich people who don't ordinarily go to a church to hear a message but they'd go shopping," he says. "And this is just my way of presenting the Gospel to them, through what they do. Hopefully they can find God through a T-shirt."

As if Kraft doesn't have enough on his plate, he's also working on the Filthy Rags Agency, a distribution company that will run both Christian and secular message-based lines under one roof, including graffiti artist Dave Kinsey's work. With all the projects he's got going on, he confesses he's only setting out on what God has equipped him to do; the rest is out of his hands. "I can only plant the seeds, and hope that someone waters them," he says. "Someone else reaps the harvest." —*Bobby Kim*

J.D. MYERS

AGE:24
BIRTHPLACE:BALTIMORE, MARYLAND
OCCUPATION: MUSICIAN, ACTOR

Talented enough to have already landed one record deal and on the cusp of another, J.D. Myers seems an ideal fit within the Christian music industry. Plenty of singing prowess demonstrated at his church, on his albums, and on television. Good looks. Lots of energy.

The problem is, Myers is too ambitious. He wants to reach as many people as possible with his music, and not be another recording star in the niche sky of choir-feeding Nashville. The doors are opening. Myers has spent time the past year hanging and performing with MTV favorites O-Town, singing at Britney Spears concerts, and doing the club thing—while some at his church debate whether any of it's the right thing. "I think if anything, I've shown people that at least Christians can be full of grace and mercy and acceptance," says Myers, who appeared on O-Town's MTV show *Making the Band* in January 2002. "We can be hip, we can be cool, we can be accepted by the world without compromising our beliefs. That's what I completely believe Christ was all about."

Myers' journey into mainstream music began after singing at his parents' church in Orlando and impressing someone who knew the manager of boy band 'NSync. The manager made Myers part of a new Christian group he was putting

I.AM.RELEVANT

together—a group that literally fell apart the day after the singer moved from Virginia to Orlando for the gig. Stuck without a steady job, Myers became active in youth group ministry.

He was asked to be part of a duo called Out of Blue, replacing a singer who had run afoul of the law. One album, a tour and a few teen magazine appearances later, Myers was booted out when the original singer landed back on the street. "Long story short, it was miserable," he says. "I was given the run-around."

One day he saw an ad for a *Making the Band* audition with O-Town; the winner would get to be on the show and possibly earn a record deal. Vaguely interested, Myers eventually decided against the audition.

The night before, however, Myers ran into one of O-Town's members in a bar and the two struck a chord. The next day, he agreed to accompany a friend who wanted to audition, and ended up singing himself with hardly a care as to whether he would be picked. He was. The whirlwind kicked in, with Myers in front of the "reality" TV cameras, singing songs by Michael W. Smith and Steven Curtis Chapman, and even opening up for a Spears' concert.

Myers' immersion in mainstream culture has confirmed his impression that there is a pronounced spiritual hunger found beyond the walls of the church. "I talked to one person who admitted he cries and prays at night, and is unsure of whether God will forgive him," Myers says. "He said I had a peace he didn't have, and that I obviously was looking in the right direction. I live for opportunities like that."—*John M. De Marco*

MATT
RESLIER

AGE:27
BIRTHPLACE:ORLANDO, FLORIDA
OCCUPATION:GRAPHIC ARTIST

Computer graphics artist Matt Reslier shocked his colleagues at Curious Pictures, a New York animation company. He was so energized upon returning from a missions trip to Kosovo that he burst into a meeting and regaled his coworkers with amazing tales— including one in which a blind man gets regains his sight in a small hut after receiving Christ. "Everyone was just looking at me with their mouths open," Reslier says.

Indeed the stories he tells would amaze most anyone, not just denizens of the thoroughly secular New York art and media worlds. The tale of his own conversion to Christianity, for example, includes a harrowing overdose and near-death experience, during which he had a powerful experience of God's presence. "I knew if I went to sleep, I wasn't going to wake up," Reslier says. "It got really cold. I realized that the afterlife was real, and I was going into a black void. I realized, 'Jesus is real, and I don't know Him.' It was not a good feeling. I wanted a second chance. Thank God I got one."

It took awhile for the experience to result in a conversion, Reslier says. "Then a few years later, I just gave it all up. I said, 'God if you are real, if you can use me, make me a new person.' After that, things started slowly changing." That was four years ago. Since then, he has continued his career as a graphic artist as well as his evangelism and missions work. His month-long Kosovo sojourn was followed by a trip to Mozambique, where he served a medical missionary team as a pharmacist. Reslier's faith makes him a curiosity around Curious Pictures, where he contributes to computer-designed models for animated figures. The company has worked for clients like Coca-Cola, Disney, and Reebok. Before working there, Reslier interned at MTV, where he worked on the animated series *Daria*.

Though his colleagues are perplexed by his beliefs and lifestyle, they share good times and good conversation while pursuing common pasttimes: "I go on hardcore snowboarding trips with them, in the back woods, on big ramps," Reslier says. "And whenever I get alone with one of them, I don't have to say anything; they want to know about my beliefs, and why I'm a Christian."

His missions trips are with Times Square Church, started in the 1980s by *Cross and the Switchblade* author David Wilkerson. The racially mixed congregation meets in the same Broadway playhouse that hosted the musical *Jesus Christ Superstar* in the 1970s. For the foreseeable future, however, Reslier is focusing on mission fields closer to home. He volunteers at a coffeehouse near his home called the East Harlem Fellowship, which ministers to locals whether their need is for friendship, spiritual guidance or just a good cup of coffee. There he spends time with people who have been taught that Christianity is mainly about following a set of rules. "They don't know what freedom in Christ is," he says.
—*Jenny S. Johnson*

I.AM.RELEVANT

CHERYL HARRIS SHARMAN

AGE:31
BIRTHPLACE:HOUSTON, TEXAS
OCCUPATION:WRITER, NON-PROFIT FOUNDER

Cheryl Harris Sharman doesn't mince words. From her East Harlem home, she pursues her vocation as a writer and runs Bezaleel House, a nonprofit artists-in-residence community, with characteristic passion and unflinching honesty.

In her writing, Sharman addresses controversial subjects in Christian circles: mental illness, the poor, her and husband Russell's decision not to have children. Her commitment to honestly address these topics puts her at odds with some Christian publications, so Sharman finds other outlets, including a regular book-reviewing gig with *The Miami Herald*. "I don't mind writing for believers per se, because there are some issues that need to be addressed to those in the church," Sharman says. "But so often Christian magazines and publishers fill their pages with the same authors writing to the same niche audience saying the same things. The writer who dares to say something outside [these] parameters often doesn't 'work' for that audience, not because the writing isn't penetrating, but because the audience has grown accustomed to not being penetrated."

It's this penetrating interaction with culture, along with a measure of social justice, that Sharman sought through the creation of Bezaleel House. The House was named for the master craftsman from the book of Exodus, whose story Sharman believes contains "endless lessons" for us: God "didn't just want Bezaleel to make a pine box; he wanted the best from this first master craftsman. He didn't just want Bezaleel to do the work in isolation; he called the Israelites to bring their precious jewels for the task. He didn't just want Bezaleel to be the best and use the best tools; he called him to teach others," she explains.

The House has sponsored arts classes for local kids and hosted coffeehouses where people share art and fellowship together. Here, too, Sharman tackles difficult topics including race relations, a natural in her mixed-race neighborhood. She's also committed to addressing the "unnecessary dichotomy" between "Christian" and "secular" art. This view "seems to say it can't be Christian simply because it's created by a Christian using the best tools, or even that it has to invoke His name in order to glorify (God)," she wrote. "The fallout can be the production of art that lacks relevance outside the church, falls short of the high standards of earlier Christian artists like Michelangelo or C.S. Lewis, and/or judges the faith of a particular artist like Madeleine L'Engle as suspect whenever they can't find overt references to God in their work."

Sharman doesn't set out to make people uncomfortable, but she wrote that it sometimes happens as a byproduct of pursuing her calling to truth. "My calling as a Christian doesn't ask me to make people comfortable," Sharman says. "It asks me to make people consider whether a particular view or action reflects Christ's. It isn't my intention to win the argument, or to make anyone believe what I believe; it's to hold their paradigm to the Light and see if it's true." —*Jenny S. Johnson*

BRETT MATSON

AGE:34
BIRTHPLACE:LA JOLLA, CALIFORNIA
OCCUPATION:WHATEVER SOMEONE WILL HIRE HIM TO DO

The only thing Brett Matson doesn't get is how others just don't get it. A while back he ran into some old club-promoter chums who had trouble understanding why he left the fast life to follow the Lord. "When you see a line wrapping around your venue and people having fun, do you take credit for that?" he sternly asked of the successful twentysome-things who were living the California dream. After a resounding "duh," Matson then con-tinued, "So if someone leaves the club drunk and dies in a car accident, do you accept responsibility?"

It's easy to see that Matson, otherwise known as "Bird," doesn't pull punches when it comes to dealing with accountability. That's why he ditched the single-guy paradise of drugs, money, and whatever else comes along with San Diego nightclub promotion. "Even though I thought, 'This is my life, I can do what I want, I can promote whatever I want to promote,' I saw the masses being tricked, hurt, and dying in accidents," he says. "You're trying to think, 'That's not me that's doing that,' but I had to be held accountable for what I did and that changed what I decided to promote."

After Bird gave everything to Christ less than a decade ago, he set out to promote a more positive environment for San Diego young adults who were stuck with few options for entertainment: Melting Pot. "You're either in the club scene or you're out of it. If you're not into it, you're bored out of your mind," he explains. "Melting Pot came about by trying to be sober in a world where there's no place to hang out if you're sober. There are a lot of people saying, 'Stay sober, don't do this, don't do that,' but they don't tell us what we *can* do or where we can go."

Every Monday night in the hyper-rich, yet bleak, beachfront community of La Jolla, Melting Pot convenes in an abandoned art gallery. Surrounded by post-pop paintings and black-and-white stills, musical artists from local favorites to 4th Avenue Jones compete for the crowd's attention. With so few venues promoting good music and culture without shoving bottles down throats and emptying wallets, Melting Pot attracts a diverse crowd of both Christian and non-Christian high-schoolers, pro surfers, and the artsy fartsy. In a nation where Sunday morning is the most segregated time of the week, that's what Bird envisioned when he named his multi-media event. "If anyone should represent diversity and begin change, it should be the church," he says.

Speaking of church and change, Bird says, "Church has been seen as an eclectic group of people that just couldn't fit in anywhere else, but the Greek word for church is 'ecclesia' which means 'the called out community,' and that sounds more like a revolution," he says. "Christians were the ones who were the movers and shakers and now, we've removed ourselves from politics, etc. It's not just the separation of church and state, it's the separation of church and public. We can't separate ourselves; we should be involved in everything."
—Bobby Kim

CASEY JEAN NOLAND

AGE:23
BIRTHPLACE:SAN LUIS OBISPO, CALIFORNIA
OCCUPATION:CAGE FIGHTER, KICK BOXER

What would it take for you to lock yourself in a ten-foot-tall cage with a blood-thirsty enemy who's just waiting to use every street fighting move possible to knock you to the ground? You've got nothing but your bare hands to survive. And after they slam the cage shut, there are only two ways out: you're either pulled up off the floor or you march out victorious.

Only legal in a handful of states (like Nevada, Connecticut, and New Jersey) and on Indian reservations in California, cage fighting has gained underground momentum across America. Envision a platform the size of a boxing ring, surrounded on all sides by nothing but a black chain link fence. Once inside, fighters use a mix of kickboxing and wrestling techniques to beat or choke their opponent into submission or knock them unconscious.

It may sound worse than a scene from *Fight Club*. And sometimes it is. But for Casey Jean Noland, a twenty-three year old kickboxing instructor, college senior, and single mother, it's a way of life. "My family thinks I'm crazy," she says, laughing. "I guess they're just scared for me."

So why does a smart, beautiful woman willingly involve herself in something so dangerous?

Noland has always been highly athletic and competitive. In her teens, she won countless kickboxing and martial arts tournaments. When cage fighting surfaced in the nineties, it offered Noland unprecedented ways to combine her skills. "The sport is so extreme, everything is taken to a higher level: your adrenaline, your athleticism," she says.

To Noland, fighting isn't fueled by anger. And it doesn't always require inflicting pain. Fighting is a sport that demands skill. "I pray for my opponent's safety every time I compete," she says. "I'm not there to give a bloody, entertaining show by beating on the other girl's face. There are other ways to end the fight—wrestling holds, ground moves—that will cause my opponent the least amount of pain and still allow me to win."

Noland admits she's lost some fights because she doesn't have that "I-want-to-hurt-you-mentality." But the hours spent training are never wasted. "It's really about the close relationships I've built with my teammates and trainers, who all know I'm a Christian and respect my faith. My teammates are like a family to me. We all look out for each other. Because I fight, I'm good friends with people who wouldn't normally spend time with Christians. I'm constantly reminded to pray for them and challenged to live out my faith in visible ways. Hopefully they see who I am, and I have a positive influence in their life."

When she's out of the cage, Noland is also able to form mentor relationships with the women in her kickboxing classes. "I think it's important for women to have strong role models," she says. Every week, she's able to teach other women confidence and help build their self-esteem through the discipline of martial arts. —*Jennifer Ashley*

JAMIE THOMAS

AGE:27
BIRTHPLACE:MELBOURNE, FLORIDA
OCCUPATION:PROFESSIONAL SKATEBOARDER, SKATEBOARD COMPANY ENTREPRENEUR

There's something that drives young adults to skateboarding. For some, it's an after-school activity, a sport, or a pop-culture trend. For others, a skateboard embodies anarchy, tough questions, and an outlet for independent thinkers. Jamie Thomas, arguably one of the most phenomenal skateboarders today, is a shoe-in for the latter.

Raised in Alabama, those questions were formulated early in his life. "I grew up going to church in a conservative town," he says. "It's really pressed upon you that you have to believe in God; you're almost forced to believe, because if you don't you're such a bad seed that you're alienated. I drifted away and started making my own conclusions, searching for my own identity." Thomas pensively continues, "As a teenager, I was rebelling against everything, but as I progressed and matured I stopped arguing against religion and tried to feel comfortable with where I was. But you're never too comfortable without God. There's always a void or emptiness there that you really never can figure out."

After several heartfelt debates with his wife, who is a Christian, Thomas began to open his heart to the possibility of truth in Christ, eventually opening his eyes to the glory of God after a series of emotional battles. As word got out that a skateboarding legend had come to Christ, youth pastors everywhere began to track him down.

"In the first year it started getting out there, I started getting loads of requests to speak," Thomas recounts. "I didn't know anything about speaking and I barely knew where I was in my faith. I found myself burning out. In the beginning, you feel like you're obligated to serve the Lord in ways other people see fit. It takes a couple scenarios to see that it's not the will of the Lord. It's the will of man driving you and pulling you in different directions." At times, he felt disheartened with their motives. "I really appreciate what people are doing when they're spreading the Gospel," he says. "But when they see someone out there as a way to get something accomplished for their own satisfaction, that's when it goes sour."

Now, three years later, Thomas has learned to balance God's plans for his life. He runs Black Box Distribution, which houses top-notch skateboard companies. He's also wrapping up Zero's newest skate video, *Dying to Live*, a project he holds dear because this time, he's says he's doing it for the Lord, not Jamie Thomas. "I feel like every time I tried to take all the credit myself I felt emptier and emptier," he says. He ponders a moment before adding, "I feel like if everything I do doesn't somehow reflect the glory of God, even if it's something very few see, I feel like I'm just resorting back to my old selfish ways."
—Bobby Kim

I.AM.RELEVANT

MARK SCANDRETTE

AGE:30
BIRTHPLACE:HEIDELBERG, GERMANY
OCCUPATION:NON-PROFIT CO-FOUNDER

Spend any time in discussion with Mark Scandrette, and your ears will be seasoned with words like "culture," "art," "prayer," "creatives," "gay and lesbian," "Jesus," "lifestyle," "service," "community," "family," "heroin addicts," and "worship." Some of those words help describe Scandrette, a devoted and passionate follower of Christ. Other words describe the environment he lives and works in—the heart of San Francisco.

The world Scandrette creates through efforts like Re/IMAGINE! is both powerful and peculiar. Re/IMAGINE! is a non-profit organization in San Francisco that fuels initiatives that integrate Christian spiritual formation, social action, community building, and the creative process. While the events he organizes to support both the arts and the local community are monumental, those compositions must be built brick by brick in the relationships of his everyday life.

A recent conversation:

Neighbor: "I don't understand what the big deal is about marriage. My girlfriend and I have been together for six years."

Mark: "I think marriage is an amazing thing. I believe we were made to love someone for a lifetime. The commitment of marriage provides security for the relationship. And it builds character to love someone over the long-term—rather than moving on when loving gets difficult."

Neighbor: "I guess I'm afraid of commitment. What if a better Mrs. Right comes along? Hey, so are you religious?"

Mark: "Absolutely not. But I'm very spiritual."

Neighbor: "So you are religious?"

Mark: "No, we are really into discovering how to live in the life and teachings of Jesus. In every time and place there are earnest people who want to experience the fresh reality of God in their lives—and that is what we want to be about."

Neighbor: "Well, my best friend is getting religious. He's getting married, and the girl he's marrying is religious. They have been thinking about going to church, and he has quit drinking. He won't drink with me at parties anymore. Now he only takes Ecstasy and snorts cocaine."

Later, while visiting a garage sale, Scandrette recognizes a woman sitting on the sidewalk. As they begin to talk she starts to cry. "My two-month-old baby died last night," she says. Her husband approaches, and Scandrette consoles them and asks to pray with them. Scandrette, his own son Noah, and the couple huddle together in a circle crying and praying together. Over the next few days he assembles a support network, visits the couple in the residential hotel where they live, go with them to the county coroner's office to view the baby's body, and helps make funeral arrangements. This is the life and influence of Mark Scandrette, an artist painting with broad strokes of life.—*Daniel Miller*

I.AM.RELEVANT

CATHY PAINE

AGE:33
BIRTHPLACE:SOUTH AFRICA
OCCUPATION:CREATIVE DIRECTOR, PROPHETIK

You're browsing through a gritty clothing store called Lucky 13 in Los Angeles. Shelved between leather and spikes, you find a fitted long sleeve shirt with three words across the front: "freedom from religion." You shell out a 10 spot, throw the shirt on, and stop by your friend Derek's house—where you find him on the bathroom floor, needle between the veins in his left foot.

"Freedom from religion, man. It's about time you got off that Jesus trip." These are his words as you turn to leave. But then the back of your shirt catches his eye. He asks you to wait up and then starts reading out loud: "Religion: the act of playing church. Substituting ritual for reality. Mindlessly following the traditions of men (rules, regulations, condemnation, performance) instead of pursuing friendship with God."

The next day, Derek asks you questions about what it's like, pursuing a friendship with God. After a few conversations, his world is shaken. He calls to tell you he just got down on his knees and offered his life to Christ. He really believes for the first time.

True encounters like these are exactly why Cathy Paine co-founded Prophetik, an urban clothing line that features subtle graphics and intriguing text about faith, Jesus, and even disturbing realities like the sex-slave trades going on in Bangkok.

"My vision for Prophetik is to make clothes that really get people in conversations, shirts that are actually intriguing and not cheesy or offensive like so much else out there," she says. In her beautiful South African accent, Paine explains her biggest frustration: for years, the Gospel has been so poorly packaged, people aren't discovering what's inside. Whether it's a second rate hat or a book cover that makes passers-by cringe, Paine knows it's time Christians start marketing Jesus in a convincing way. "It's not like we're selling an empty container," she says. "The inside of the package is the most beautiful and life-changing, but people aren't even opening it up."

Set out to change that, Paine and her small team travel to fashion trade shows like Magic in Las Vegas, where urban retailers are quick to snatch up shirts with what Prophetik calls their "wearable philosophy." [TM] "I want each shirt to be a clever, cultural container for the gospel that someone who doesn't believe in God can pick up, be intrigued by, and consider the meaning within it," she says. Skipping the Christian market, Paine wants her street wear to attract the every day teen who is in search of something meaningful.

With the unending support of her husband, Paine has also been involved in promoting catch-fire movements like The Call (a twelve-hour day of fasting and prayer in urban centers like Boston and New York that's attracting hundreds of thousands at each event). She's co-authored two books, *Digging the Wells of Revival* and *Fast Forward.* And at Prophetik, her passion for activism continues through the generous support of ministries who help mis-treated women worldwide. —*Jennifer Ashley*

I.AM.RELEVANT

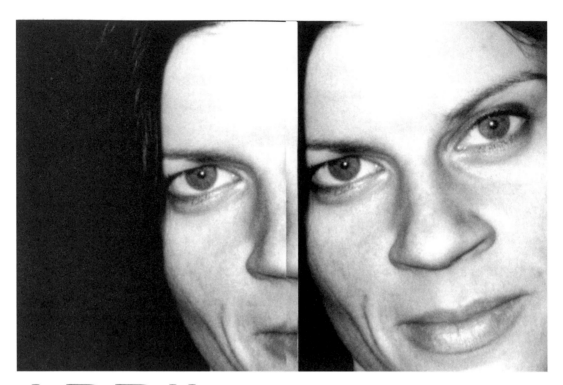

APRIL WOODS

AGE:31
BIRTHPLACE:LANCASTER, CALIFORNIA
OCCUPATION:MASSAGE THERAPIST, ESTHETICIAN

The elderly Jewish man was crying, but he didn't know why. April Woods, his massage therapist, knew. It was the prayer for him she raised to God that moved him, one of many she has offered over the years during his weekly visits to her studio.

Woods has offered the presence of Christ to all she has encountered since her early days at beauty school, when she'd bring her Bible along for a little personal quiet time during breaks. "I started having forty-year-old women coming up to me with their problems, thinking about getting a divorce, and wondering what I thought about it," she says.

Woods served the same function for her clients when she switched to the hair business. "I was taking clients out back door and just praying with them," she says. "I had one client with two young daughters, and I felt led to start taking them to church. Their mom was farthest thing from a Christian ... one of them wound up becoming saved."

Though most clients were receptive to Woods, one coworker wasn't. He'd been treating her harshly and Woods asked whether he had a problem with her. "I'm so tired of hearing you talk about God this, and God that," he told her. "I'm sick of hearing it." Woods adds, "When you love God and love taking about Him, that's what cuts you to the core."

Since opening her own business offering massages and facials in 1996, Woods has felt free to express her faith in the ways God leads her to. "It's great to have that freedom to minister, because they're in there for therapy and to feel better," she says. "It's so awesome to be able to lay hands on clients and pray for them." It's a ritual she performs at the end of each massage. "Though they're not always Christians, sometimes they can sense what I'm doing, and they say, 'Amen,'" says Woods, even though she usually prays silently.

Not afraid to follow God's leading in her life, Woods has done everything from engage with a client who practices witchcraft to giving a copy of *The Ragamuffin Gospel* to a non-Christian client she believed would connect with the book. "I know God has these specific people in my life, and there's no way they're not going to be saved, because God's got them so heavily on my heart," she says.

Next she plans to reach out to the kids from the alternative school who attend the YMCA where she works out. "God's been laying it on my heart to start inviting those kids to our youth group," she says. "If God's given you a heart for that, it's all kids, not just the ones you know."

Woods and her husband, drummer for the Terry Kelly band, are youth group leaders at their church. Woods works with young women, imparting to them the lesson she lives out in her own life: "They don't have to go into the ministry to live a life that's like Christ."
—*Jenny S. Johnson*

HEATHER MCDONALD

AGE:29
BIRTHPLACE:TRICITIES, WASHINGTON
OCCUPATION:PHOTOGRAPHER

Heather McDonald stopped the offices of the Ford Modeling Agency cold in their tracks. She had worked for them as a models' photographer for about two years, when somebody asked her a question, "I don't even remember what, but it was a perfect opportunity to share the Lord," she says. "The whole entire office stopped what they were doing and listened."

McDonald has been a Christian for nine years, since realizing the things she was filling her life with, including photography, friends, clubs, and drugs, were not fulfilling her. "I realized one day that it didn't matter what I was doing, who I was with, or how much money I was making; I was in need," she recalls. Neighbors invited her to a Bible study, and she says it was there she was "like a dry sponge that someone was pouring water on. God filled that void that nothing else could fill."

During those early days, McDonald says, "before I started to get really grounded in the Lord, I would totally compromise" when confronted with situations that offended her Christian convictions. "I was too afraid to tell them I was a Christian," she says. "But the Spirit of God changed me from being afraid to offend anyone in my work, to not really caring what people think anymore and being able to be open with people about the Lord."

I.AM.RELEVANT

That openness has resulted in a wide range of relationships for McDonald, and opportunities to serve people she works with and around. "I've had a lot of divine appointments," she says. "I travel a lot, working in all the big cities, and usually, everywhere I go, I find consistently that there is always a Christian that I meet or one special person that will stick out on a job where I can plant a seed, be a light."

McDonald says her difficult past enables her to reach people in the fashion industry. "I'm perfect by no means," she says. "But God is so good in that He uses my failures. I'm not that super squeaky-clean person. Just saying, 'Hey, this is where I've come from and this is what I've done,' makes me relatable."

McDonald says light is in short supply in her business. "There's a lot of snarlyness; it's a very dark industry," she says. "I am a light in a dark place." And that's a big reason she stays in the industry, though she may get frustrated with its darker side. "I'll pray, 'God, if you don't want me in this business, close the door,'" she says. "Then in one week, I'll work with two Christians, two who are searching for the Lord, and one seeker. I feel like God is affirming, 'I want you right where you are.'"—*Jenny S. Johnson*

RICH
HIRSCH

AGE:22
BIRTHPLACE:SEATTLE, WASHINGTON
OCCUPATION:PROFESSIONAL BMX RIDER

Burnside, Portland. Show up at 7 A.M.—an ungodly hour in the BMX community—to get a good session in before the skaters show up. Be ready to step over stinky bums, nasty vomit, and smoking trashcans.

Built illegally after dark by trespassing skaters and later sanctioned by the city as an official skate park, the grafittied concrete and crumbling cinderblock walls under the rusty Burnside Bridge have become a landmark of anti-establishment ingenuity. And that's exactly where you'll find Rich Hirsch.

At twenty-two he's already gone pro, with several sponsors like Vans and Mosh to keep him living the BMX life. And he's already launched a successful business, Salvation Clothing Company, that's doing well enough to sponsor four other Christian riders besides himself.

But a few years ago, Hirsch didn't think any of this could be possible. After a bad fall that tore his ACL and months of seeing specialists without getting any answers, he was left with the conclusion that getting back on his bike was out of the question.

"I started riding at fifteen, so for four years, that was my life," he says. "I lived and breathed BMX. Then, out of nowhere, I lost everything that I thought was important to me. For an entire year, I was mad and depressed. It was a very low point for me."

During this time, Hirsch moved in with his dad, a Christian man who never pressed religion on his kids, but encouraged them to question and decide for themselves. "But over that year, piece by piece God was putting me back together. I started accepting the fact He did care for me and that there was something larger in life than BMX."

Now that his body has healed, Hirsch lives with a fierce humility: an awareness that everything could be taken away again. But he carries a look of contentment. "I'm going to ride for as long as my body will let me," he says. "And every time I go down a handrail or some tricky stairs, I know it's only possible because God is allowing it. I'm out there to ride for Him and to let people know that He has given me everything that I have: a chance to ride again and to do it professionally, a chance to make a life out of what I love."

One subtle way Hirsch lets other BMX riders know about his faith is through Salvation Clothing Company, which he started a year ago. With the simple word Salvation splayed across hoodies, beanies, and T-shirts, Hirsch is able to combat the other prevalent image tattooed on a lot of BMX gear: 666, stitched in fiery red on clothing made by a company called Little Devil. "With Salvation, I'm able to offer an option so people can turn in the other direction. Now riders, especially younger kids, email me every day. They're stoked to find an older Christian who rides and a company that reflects their beliefs."
—*Jennifer Ashley*

I.AM.RELEVANT

KANTEN RUSSELL

AGE:28
BIRTHPLACE:LINCOLN, NEBRASKA
OCCUPATION:PROFESSIONAL SKATEBOARDER

Pro skateboarder Kanten Russell leaps off thirty-foot flights of stairs multiple times a day. Voluntarily. On a piercingly sunny day in Clairmont, California, Russell says, "My strength training specialist basically told me there are certain people that are genetically built to be able to handle that kind of stuff without getting beat up too much … and I am one of them."

Well, then, it seems this brother's chosen the right J.O.B. For the past eight years, Russell has professionally spearheaded the globally pervasive movement otherwise known as skateboarding. He's one of Osiris Shoes' headlining names and along with fellow skateboarder Dave Mayhew, founded Elenex Clothing last year. His face, along with his mind-boggling backside 180s down behemoth gaps, can readily be found in magazines, videos, and television. And with skateboarding's steady departure from Southern California "bro" sport to its niche as the foremost youth subculture/multi-million-dollar industry, Russell's been learning to accept his position in the new school of rock stars.

"I've heard them actually arguing outside my door before about who's gonna ring the door-bell," he says in reference to the throngs of teenage admirers who accost him on a daily basis. "Even on Halloween, there were three girls there, I told them I didn't have much candy, they said, 'That's okay, we just wanted to know if you were Kanten Russell.'"

Yet, for Russell, his gifts in skateboarding have a far greater purpose than signature shoes and autograph sessions—it's a witnessing tool. "Not only is skateboarding fun for me and supporting my family, but I can actually talk to the kids and reach out to them too. Using my life not only for myself but using skateboarding to minister to kids and as a tool for God, just giving back to God what He's given to me," he explains.

Not surprisingly, Russell himself came to know the Lord through skateboarding. Years ago, skate videographer Dave Schlossbach would relentlessly ask of Russell, "You already tried it your way, why don't you try it God's way? If you ever want to go back the other way, go right ahead," he recalls. "But Dave guaranteed that I'd be happier living my life with Jesus in it. So I accepted Christ."

These days, Russell discerns the importance of reaching younger generations in their environment, instead of preaching down to them. "To reach kids these days I don't think you can just walk into a chapel and have them psyched to get saved. You need to be more youth-oriented. If you can't even get someone's interest, how are they going to hear the Word? A lot of pastors around the country are understanding that and organizing a lot more events now utilizing more youth-oriented music and sports that would have never been in a church parking lot. If you don't adapt and reach kids at that level, then you're never gonna get them to come to God and understand that Jesus is just a relationship and it's for everybody, not just those forty and over."—*Bobby Kim*

SHANE GILBERT

AGE:30
BIRTHPLACE:DENVER, COLORADO
OCCUPATION:PRODUCER, WRITER

Shane Gilbert isn't afraid to quote a green frog. She says her dream to work in Hollywood began at the age of seven when she watched *The Muppet Movie* for the first time. "Every element of Miss Piggy, Kermit, and Fozzie packing up the old Studebaker and following their dreams to Hollywood still feed my dreams now," she says. "So, I think this entire Hollywood thing may have started then. Kermit's inspiring words still haunt me: 'Life's like a movie, write your own ending, keep believing, keep pretending … the lovers, the dreamers, and me.'"

After graduating from Texas Christian University where she majored in creative writing and world religions, Gilbert moved to a small ski resort town and began teaching AP literature and working as a college counselor for six years. She spent her days lecturing smart kids on what it means to venture out into the world and be somebody, to make this one life count for everything God intends it to be. Her weekends were spent writing screenplays and watching movies.

"One day, I think I finally got sick of listening to my own lectures on fictitious characters who misspent their lives—I took a two week sabbatical to think and pray about moving to Hollywood," she says. "Then, I remembered Kermit and Fozzie and I took the leap of faith, with no savings, no job, no plan—just friends and a futon to sleep on."

In the fall of 2000, Gilbert moved to Burbank, California, and began pursuing her dream. She worked at PAX-TV as an executive assistant where she learned about television and film. Then a budget cut and severance package allowed her enough time and money to do what she really wanted. In April of 2001, she founded Sodium Entertainment, a TV/film development company, with two partners. They currently work on all kinds of projects including writing cartoon episodes, filming DVD productions, developing new TV pilots and promoting high profile Olympic athletes.

Gilbert still holds onto her dream of standing in front of the Academy and reciting her acceptance speech for Best Screenplay, but over the last few years, she's started to recognize she has a different gifting. "I don't think my gift isn't to be the best anything—I get things started and I encourage others and help them get started," she says. "And now I know that's the job description of a Hollywood producer. So, I guess I'm a producer, I start things. I psyche other people up—some may question if that's actually a job."

Hollywood isn't always easy on Gilbert or anyone else. Over the last year and a half, she's already seen a lot of people come and go. Yet Gilbert is still holding on. "A lady once told me, 'If you spend one to two years of your life following your dream, then there are only two outcomes: One, either you fail and you spend the rest of life knowing that you weren't meant to do it. Or two, you succeed and you never regret the change."—*Margaret Feinberg*

RANDALL GODFREY

AGE:28
BIRTHPLACE:VALDOSTA, GEORGIA
OCCUPATION:PROFESSIONAL FOOTBALL PLAYER

The two things most associated with Sunday are probably football and church. A few years back, two of those went head-to-head for Randall Godfrey when he signed on with the Tennessee Titans as starting linebacker—a contract that culminated decades of hard work, passion, and faith.

Born and bred in Valdosta, an unassuming town in the heart of the South, a professional football career was more of a storybook dream then a plausible reality for the six-foot, two-inch star athlete. Yet for Godfrey, drive and determination overshadowed any apprehension that dared hinder him from pursuing God's plan for his life. "I just loved sports, period," he remembers. "Most days I'd come home, do my homework, and I'm out doing football. I knew this was what I wanted to do; I didn't know how far I could go. I was just committed to being the best I could be, and I made it to the NFL."

For many youngsters who share Godfrey's endzone dream, it all comes crashing down as a result of falling in with the wrong crowd, losing sight of that potential future at the hands of drugs, gangs, etc. It's a truth Godfrey was faced with and overcame himself. "A lot of it I pay tribute to my parents," he says. "We come back from a Christian family and my mom is a schoolteacher and my dad works with the sheriff's department. I come from a very disciplined family, so while playing football I had to really focus on staying out of trouble and having good grades. Anytime I got off track or something happened they always threatened to take football away from me. That was the biggest challenge, so it didn't make things easy at all."

He still relies on others to hold him accountable in a profession that is wrought with over-the-top hedonism: young males at the top of their game with big money, front-page glamour, and alluring women. "You gotta be strong," Godfrey says. "I'm twenty-eight years old now but the peer pressure's still out there. You just gotta know when to say when and the good thing about it is you gotta surround yourself with other Christians. I don't hang out with guys who get in trouble a lot, I try to associate myself with God-fearing men who go out and do positive things."

Now Godfrey is living his dream and gives God all the credit. "The main thing is you have to thank God for giving you the opportunity to fulfill a dream, to get paid to do something you love to do. A lot of people have jobs but its something they really didn't want to do, they just happened to be put in that position, but I'm doing something I love doing, getting paid to do it and I'm very thankful that the Lord blessed me … I just thank Him every Sunday I step on that field to have what I have and to take care of my family."—*Bobby Kim*

I.AM.RELEVANT

JEREMY LIMPIC

AGE:25
BIRTHPLACE:REDLANDS, CALIFORNIA
OCCUPATION:GRAPHIC DESIGNER

Last year, P.O.D.'s "Alive" scored as the most-played video on MTV and captivated viewers with stunning cinematography. Yet, for many, one image comes to mind in association with the landmark video, a pierced hand emblazoned onto singer Sonny Sandoval's T-shirt.

That icon was property of onetruth.com and was more than enough for Jeremy Limpic who, as owner of San Luis Obispo-based onetruth.clothing, watched his indie company explode into pop culture. "We suddenly found ourselves in the position of being somewhat trendy," Limpic says, "but we always need to remember that when it's said and done, no one will remember onetruth.com, and rightfully so."

Those humble remarks are rooted in humble beginnings. Born in Southern California, Limpic moved with his missionary parents to Brazil at the age of nine, a transition that was far from comfortable. "In Brazil I'm a 'gringo.' Here in the U.S. I feel Brazilian. So I don't feel completely at home in either place, but then again I feel at home in both." Confused? "I guess it fits in to the whole idea of finding our identity in Christ anyway, I mean we are supposed to be 'aliens and strangers' in this world," Limpic says.

Before he found that identity in Christ, Limpic moved back to the States to attend college, and searched for fulfillment through the party scene. He eventually ditched the lifestyle after immersing himself in the straight-edge subculture ("It was a big deal for me to see tough, tattooed men yelling and screaming about purity, unity, and positive action"), ultimately paving his way to Christ. "In the straight-edge scene, clothing is really important in expressing who you are, so it was logical for me to want to express what Christ had done in my life through my clothing." He recalls, "Nothing I found at my friendly Christian bookstore really expressed what God had done in my life … they just weren't me. I didn't have much affinity for pink puffy paint saying 'Jesus Saves' or a shirt with a big bloody cross saying 'This Blood's for You' or something like that. So I ended up making my own shirts."

Along with friend and partner Billy Itzen, the two have been tirelessly progressing the message of the one and only Truth amid full-time college careers, occupations, and marriage (Limpic's, to wife, Beth). Also an accomplished web and graphic designer, Limpic never sees much of a profit from his ministry, funneling every onetruth penny back into onetruth, a mentality that may seem discouraging considering the company is perpetually in the hole and the reality that he could easily wallow in his good fortune. But Limpic finds little worth in worldly riches; instead he concentrates on eternal blessings. "Our prayer is that the message that God has burned into our hearts and that we have screened onto the shirts will somehow be used through the power of the Holy Spirit to change eternal destinies. And that's where we find our satisfaction. Nothing beats the pleasure of God over a saved life."—*Bobby Kim*

JULIA DYER

AGE:24
BIRTHPLACE:SAN JOSE, CALIFORNIA
OCCUPATION:ENVIRONMENTAL SCIENTIST

When Julia Dyer took a job as a water quality specialist, who knew she'd be sneaking around underground Methamphetamine labs on the back roads of California.

One of her first assignments led her to a town a few hours north of Santa Barbara to collect water samples. As she was leaving, her wheels started spinning in the mud, so she hopped out the truck to find a plank from a nearby barn, only to be stopped by three tenants, who as Dyer recalls, "were so sweet, they wouldn't let me lift a finger."

After they gracefully shooed her off the property, Dyer discovered they were only being helpful so she wouldn't discover the meth lab they were operating in their house. Dyer remembers, "It was scary because they were cooking up strong chemicals in such a confined space; the whole house could have blown while I was touring the land!"

Even if her job requires her to trek through some dangerous territory, this twenty-four year old will continue to do whatever it takes to protect the landscape.

"My true passion is actually animals," Dyer says over coffee and backgammon. "But to make a lasting impact in helping wildlife, I have to protect their habitats. So, I turned my focus to land resource management and water quality."

Dyer has discovered being a Christian and being an environmentalist is not a popular combination in the realm of office politics. "Just this week, my cube-mate bluntly admitted he couldn't believe I actually called myself a scientist, since I'm not also an evolutionist. I ended our conversation by pointing out that whether or not we descended from monkeys doesn't change the fact the water is still polluted. Sometimes I have to convince my officemates that we can both do our jobs and make a significant contribution, even if we have different worldviews."

Even though her faith in God and her scientific endeavors seem contradictory to her co-workers, Dyer's passion for all of God's creation—people, land, and animals—doesn't waver. "I may be the only Bible my co-workers ever read, so they all know that my environmental beliefs are fueled by my religious beliefs. I'm convinced God continues to use creation as a testimony for His existence and since nature is a place where we can meet with God in a powerful way, I believe in protecting it for future generations." —*Jennifer Ashley*

ARTS
SECTION.TWO

DAN HASELTINE

AGE:29
BIRTHPLACE:SPRINGFIELD, MASSACHUSETTS
OCCUPATION:SINGER/SONGWRITER

Faith is often an endless wrestling match, interlaced with moments of breathless struggle and triumphant pinning of God—awareness into the deeper places of the heart. Dan Haseltine, lead singer of Jars of Clay, has spent most of the past decade encouraging those within and beyond the stained glass windows to find freedom in posing the tougher questions which give a higher purpose to the struggle.

Haseltine's parents noticed his love of music at an early age and bought him a piano. On one occasion, after having learned a few songs, he spontaneously joined a jazz combo at his uncle's wedding reception and impressed the guests. "One of the things they noticed was at ten years old, I was already listening to the band and following the drummer," he said.

Haseltine played in some garage bands as a teenager. Although he hadn't listened to a lot of Christian music, Haseltine joined his church's worship team in junior and senior high. It seemed like a natural progression from there to attend a Christian college, he says. Upon starting classes at Greenville College to pursue a degree in contemporary Christian music, he met Matt Odmark, Charlie Lowell, and Steve Mason, with whom he began to make music. Says Haseltine, "We all kind of had the same questions going through our minds—such as why doesn't Christian music sound like mainstream music? Why can't we find many bands that seem to be as good?"

The foursome entered some competitions, including Nashville's Gospel Music Association Spotlight contest, which they won in 1994. A record deal with Essential Records followed, and in 1995 Jars of Clay's self-titled debut exploded across the charts and within the minds and hearts of Christian—and eventually mainstream—music listeners. In 2002, the band released its fourth album, *The Eleventh Hour*, and its creativity and journey into the struggles of faith have not ceased but intensified.

.MORE ›

I.AM.RELEVANT

DAN HASELTINE

"We received so much backlash from the church because of that, it really forced us to study and develop our reasons for why we were out there."

I.AM.RELEVANT

| | | | |

During their first major tour, their single "Flood" released to mainstream radio, and Haseltine and his bandmates decided to spend their "days off" playing some bars and clubs in conjunction with secular radio stations. "We received so much backlash from the church because of that, it really forced us to study and develop our reasons for why we were out there," Haseltine says. "It was a huge growing process for us—for a lot of that season, we were trying to please everybody, and were practically killing ourselves."

Haseltine says the band finally realized it would always be criticized and decided to rely on the good counsel of close friends or mentors while maintaining confidence in God's call. After that first mega tour, Haseltine and Jars decided to no longer play in churches on a regular basis, but in neutral venues such as arenas, theaters, fairs—"places where people aren't threatened. It's scary for a non-Christian to walk into a church," Haseltine says.

In the trenches of mainstream culture's hot spots, Haseltine and the other Jars members create a safe atmosphere for tumbling onto the wrestling mats.—*John M. De Marco*

DALLAS JENKINS

AGE:26
BIRTHPLACE:LAKE FOREST, ILLINOIS
OCCUPATION:MOVIE PRODUCER

Dallas Jenkins had never set foot on a movie set before gathering a director, cast, and crew in Alabama to film the $2 million movie, *Hometown Legend*. The twenty-six-year-old producer didn't know what to expect— only that this was exactly where he wanted to be. He had been in love with movies since the eighth grade when his father, best-selling author Jerry Jenkins, showed him *One Flew Over the Cuckoos Nest*. "I inherited my desire to tell stories from my father," he says. "Maybe I'm an attention freak, but I've always loved to get responses out of people."

After graduating from Northwestern College with a drama degree, Jenkins began working for Namesake Entertainment, a Christian movie production company. As he learned about the movie business and saw the quality difference between some of the evangelistic movies coming out and the best that Hollywood had to offer, he came to believe Christians should be making better movies. He went to his father with the idea to start Jenkins Entertainment.

"He wanted to light a candle rather than curse the darkness," his father says. "We've got a message, and nobody knows how to tell it. And [Dallas] said we need to have a company where you make great films—and they all aren't overtly evangelistic or 'Christian films,' but with a

I.AM.RELEVANT

Christian worldview and positive values—and show that you can do it right."

Jenkins found a script that jumped out to him—a story about tradition, pride, and being part of something bigger than yourself. It wasn't overtly religious but its message was one he firmly believed in. "The main character is a loner," he says. "He's an outsider, and he has to learn there are people who love him, there's a God who loves him, and he can be part of a team, part of a community—something he's never had before. Obviously all those things are Christian values but by no means is this a spiritually driven film or a Christian film."

In the course of a week, he obtained the rights to the script, bought a house and found out that his wife was pregnant with their first child. "I didn't feel like an adult," he says, "but I felt like adulthood came after me. I still feel like a kid doing all this crazy stuff."

He was forced to grow up quickly on the set, as the movie was plagued by a steady stream of disasters. Twice X-rays ruined portions of the film during shipping back to Los Angeles. He had to fly the actors and crew back in for extra days of shooting, further straining an already tight budget. Then in the editing room, he was bit in the face by the editor's dog, necessitating 55 stitches and cosmetic surgery. "Somehow God brought me through it," he says. But despite the difficulties, he's already planning his next movie, even as he continues to promote the first one. It will be a Christmas story written by his father called *Twas the Night Before.—Josh Jackson*

BRANDON EBEL

AGE: 31
BIRTHPLACE: DALLAS, TEXAS
OCCUPATION: FOUNDER OF TOOTH AND NAIL RECORDS

It shouldn't be news in certain circles that Christian music is not considered cool. Christians lament the quality of music that celebrates Christ, and non-Christians ignore (or worse, mock) music with Christian messages or themes. Brandon Ebel is helping to change that. By founding Tooth and Nail Records, Ebel helps foster the music of bands who have both musical integrity and Christian convictions.

Growing up, Ebel noticed the lack of quality Christian music. But it wasn't until a DJing job at Oregon State University that he began aspiring to get into the music business. After college, he got a job with Frontline Records in Southern California, spent his time attending shows by groups like Focused, Unashamed, and Wish For Eden, and wondered why they weren't signed to a label. He wanted to change things.

And change them he did. The record label he started in his one-room apartment in 1993 has become a major success story and has proved the viability of truly alternative

Christian music. From lean beginnings ("I was eating two BRCs (bean, rice, and cheese burritos) a day—and that was it," Ebel says), Tooth and Nail has expanded to fill a 7,000 square foot office space in Seattle, with offices in several other states. The business includes several labels, including Uprok which, as Ebel put it, "is expanding the market for genuinely good Christian rap music, a genre which has been lean till now.

"I love the church, and have always been supportive of quality Christian music—my own personal record collection would attest to that," Ebel says. "I just saw all of these great Christian bands that the older Christian labels weren't signing, and that had something to say to the world. I wanted to give them the opportunity to do so."

Tooth and Nail not only supports Christians making good music, but fosters community among (mostly) young people who believe Christian commitment and artistic achievement are far from mutually exclusive. Ebel is justifiably proud of the reach many have had: "Our bands' music has had an influence on the general market scene, from tours with larger acts (Project 86 with P.O.D., for example), to artistically influencing entire new genres (Pedro the Lion, MxPx, Supertones, Stavesacre, Danielson Family, Joy Electric, Starflyer 59). No one can say our bands aren't interested in being in the mainstream when you see people wearing our T-shirts on MTV's *The Real World* and musicians from bands like System Of A Down mentioning listening to Starflyer 59 in magazines like *Alternative Press*."

Ebel says he's often told he and his bands have smashed stereotypes of Christian musicians, and of Christians in general for people in the industry. He does this not mostly by preaching, but by being himself, a basketball, video game-playing guy with a "fervent interest in Apple computers," who just happens to be a Christian and responsible for the dissemination of some really good music.—*Jenny S. Johnson*

I.AM.RELEVANT

STEVE RUETSCHLE

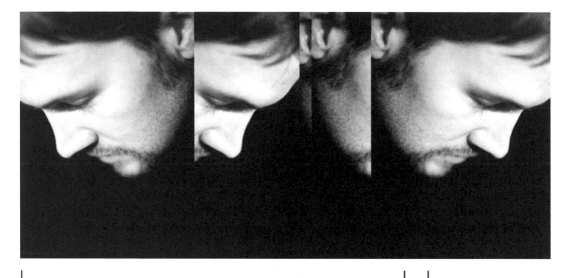

AGE:32
BIRTHPLACE:DAYTON, OHIO
OCCUPATION:ARTIST, TEACHER, COUNSELOR, WRITER, MUSICIAN

God gave Steve Ruetschle the desire and talent to do many things. While everyone encouraged him to concentrate on one area, he couldn't give up any of the things he loved. After studying Jesus' parable of the talents, he decided that to simply pick something and pursue it wasn't necessarily the biblical answer.

"I've been told time and time again—whether it's with music or visual arts—to focus, focus, focus," Ruetschle says. "I've tried all my life to focus, and I could never do it. Finally I said, 'God, You have to give me a vision that's big enough to encompass all these things because You've given me the joy from doing all these things.' It was a life-changing moment. Now I'm able to touch on a number of different things that I love." That includes serving as an adjunct professor at Mars Hill Graduate School, counseling patients in a private practice, writing books, painting, writing and recording music, and leading worship at his church.

As an illustrator, Ruetschle was working for companies like MGM and Warner Bros. while still in college. MGM hired him to reinvent the Pink Panther, giving him an updated look for the nineties. But instead of pursuing a career in graphic arts, he went to seminary, choosing a master's degree in spiritual nurturing over the more traditional Masters of Divinity track. "A lot of the people I saw coming out of seminary had the head knowledge, but lacked the perspective that they're speaking to broken hearts … real people with real issues. I wanted to be able to read the soul as well as the text. That gives way to the possibility of transformation."

During seminary, Ruetschle began leading worship for what would become Mars Hill, one of Seattle's innovative postmodern churches. He left when his band Spacefighter began touring the nation. After seven CDs and playing all the clubs made famous by Nirvana and Pearl Jam, Ruetschle continues to write songs, but performs only very occasionally. He's also in the process of publishing two children's books, *The First Christmas Present* and *Granny Takes a Walk*, and writing a book on what it means to be creative as beings made in the image of the Creator, tentatively called *Invitation to See*.

But Ruetschle is most passionate about his paintings—large eye-catching abstract designs capturing the emotion and impression left by characters in the Bible. When he wanted to learn more about the twelve apostles, he dug into Scripture and transformed the personalities of each onto twelve giant canvases. "I love to play in Scripture," he says. "I love to bring creativity to Scripture in order to transform it for me and others. I used to be bored in Scripture, and I decided to bring my joy and talents and play in them. It's transformed the Bible into a huge treasure chest and playground."

That joy is shared by those he touches in all of his pursuits. It's a big vision indeed.
—*Josh Jackson*

I.AM.RELEVANT

MARY
MARY

AGE:TWENTYSOMETHINGS
BIRTHPLACE:LOS ANGELES, CALIFORNIA
OCCUPATION:RECORDING ARTISTS

The music of Mary Mary carries a soulful, deeply spiritual sound described by some as "pure gospel" and "R&B gospel" by others. Whatever term you choose, it shouldn't come as any surprise that the two women behind the music, Erica and Tina (Tristina) Atkins, were raised by gospel-singing parents in a home where gospel songs—those by music greats such as the Clark Sisters, the Winans, Shirley Caesar, John P. Kee, and Hezekiah Walker— were the only type of music allowed in the house.

Erica began singing at the age of five, but it took a little longer for Tina's shyness to wear off. She didn't step on stage until around the age of fifteen. For both of these women, whose father was an pastor in Inglewood, California, singing in choirs became a key part of their lives.

Recruited in 1995 as part of the Michael Matthews traveling gospel show, the sisters were given the opportunity to hone their vocal skills and earned a spot on the second Matthews play. Between the two, they went on to sing backup slots for major recording artists including Kenny Lattimore, Eric Benet, Brian McKnight, Brandy, and Terry Ellis. Along the way, they were trying to hold down jobs and complete college.

In 1996, the sisters had a chance meeting with Warryn Campbell, who collaborated on tunes with them and brought their music to his publisher, EMI Music. They quickly landed their own publishing contracts and their work became in demand among musicians and Hollywood. Their song "Dance," written and performed with Robin S., was added to the *Dr. Doolittle* soundtrack. "Let Go, Let God" was included on *The Prince of Egypt* soundtrack. And Yolanda Adams recorded two of their songs, "Time To Change" and "Yeah," on her album. The duo became the first gospel act to sign with Columbia Records.

Both sisters agree the substance of their music is based on their relationship with God. "When God gives you a talent, you use it," Tina says. "I don't think every melody is something you'd find in every church, but the story and substance is [an expression of the] relationship with the Lord in our lives."

There is a flip side to the success and fame. "It's a lot of hard work and you get lonely because you're away from the people you love," Tina says. "But when you have people who went through a great tragedy in their family and say 'Your CD got us through' or 'I listened to your song and decided I wasn't going to take my life' stuff like that is a huge boost. I'm glad we won the awards. The Grammy and [going] platinum was awesome, but if we do all that and nobody is changed then it's kind of pointless."

Erica agrees. "The testimony is what drives us," she says. "If nobody's life is changed then it's pointless. When we hear testimonies, we get really excited about that."
—*Margaret Feinberg*

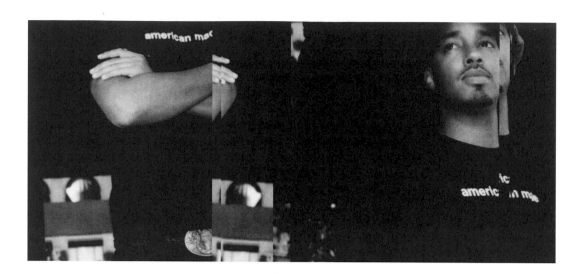

PIGEON JOHN

AGE:24
BIRTHPLACE:OMAHA, NEBRASKA
OCCUPATION:HIP-HOP ARTIST

Pigeon John has a lot to say about the Christian music industry. After all, no one's been more caught up in the crosshairs of the biz's shady corporate politics than his hip-hop outfit, LA Symphony. Tagged as one of the most promising and refreshing gigs to hit the market since Kool Herc threw down breakdowns, LA Symphony has been caught up in label bureaucracy for two years while awaiting the release of their label debut, *Call It What You Want*. Despite that, Pigeon John's story represents an exhausting journey from hip-hop devotee to leader of the new school.

Immersing himself in the world of creative writing in his mid-teens, he eventually found his way to the legendary Goodlife Cafe in the heart of Los Angeles. The club's run as an open mic hotspot from 1989 to 1994 birthed some of the most profound phenoms in modern hip-hop music (Pharcyde, Souls of Mischief), an environment that encouraged John to challenge himself as both an individual and an emcee. "I just went up there to get good. When I first got there, the response wasn't fresh, so I knew I had to get better, so every Thursday I would try to be the best person."

It wasn't long before the crowd's response got as fresh as the Fonz on a first date, prompting Pigeon John to start up side-group Brainwash Projects with BTwice, the dudes that introduced the Christian entertainment industry to the term "underground hip-hop," and later, LA Symphony. His first solo record, *Pigeon John is Clueless*, was also released under his own label, Telephone Company (keep your eyes out for his follow-up, *Pigeon John is Dating your Sister*).

As a result of their hard work, not only did John and fellow LA Symphony members strengthen as individuals and emcees, but also as Christians. "It's more challenging to live correctly rather than the outside appearance," he explains, "The more we get seen as artists, do more shows, the more the arrow points back at us and our personal lives … doing music and shows is the easy part. The hard part is living up to what we believe and what we say, whether its drinking or smoking, how we go about relationships with girl-friends, [or] how we love one another within the crew."

John's love of, well, love, may in fact be why he has such a problem with the Christian music industry. The rap aficionado contends, "In order to be successful in that arena, you basically have to be a Christian children's rock group. Everything has to be completely bla-tant, very open, very simple lyrics, a connect-the-dot situation … very easy to swallow."

In the end, John reluctantly confesses, "Sometimes I'd rather chance it in the general mar-ket and cut off the Christian market because if you blow up like Bono and say, 'I believe in Jesus Christ' blatantly, then the Christian market hugs you and loves you. But they would-n't have received you if you [had] begun honestly. I really do hate that."—*Bobby Kim*

I.AM.RELEVANT

SCOTT
STAPP

AGE:28
BIRTHPLACE:TALLAHASSEE, FLORIDA
OCCUPATION:MUSICIAN

Threesome Creed sits atop the world of rock 'n' roll these days, and dark-haired front man Scott Stapp personifies the group's angst-ridden wrestling with the deeper issues of life. While eschewing any particular labels or clichés—especially "Christian rock band"—a positive and convicting message constantly pours through Stapp's lyrics.

"At one point in my life, I thought I was called to be a minister. I think that was around nine or ten years old," Stapp says. "I became disillusioned by a lot of things that happened to me by Christian people … I wanted to get away and try to figure out things on my own, through my own study and my own search, and I'm still there. I haven't come to any resolutions."

Perhaps Stapp's acknowledgment of the open-ended nature of his faith life holds a clue to why so many young people who would never set foot in church—or at a "Christian" rock concert—resonate strongly with the ponderings of this Florida-based band. Like many others, Stapp's own experiences in church left him feeling alone in the religious crowd. "I felt like I was some big, evil sinner and I was the only one [searching], because on Sundays everyone put on their suits and sat in the front row and acted like they were perfect and had the perfect families and the perfect lives and their kids were great ... For me, to have these feelings and thoughts and have no one to identify with just isolated me more in an environment where I was supposed to feel love, understanding, and compassion," he says.

Creed burst onto the rock scene with 1997's *My Own Prison* and its provocative title track in which Stapp describes the burden of sin and the freedom of the cross. The debut yielded a record four No. 1 rock singles, and was followed in 1999 by *Human Clay* and the hits "With Arms Wide Open" (which inspired a foundation of the same name, headed by Stapp, that seeks to foster healthy child-parent relationships) and "Higher."

In late 2001 Creed released its third CD, *Weathered*. The album debuted at the top of the charts and held that position for several months. Like its predecessors, it is chock full of spiritual metaphors that could be interpreted in a variety of ways.

Stapp and his bandmates have consistently avoided interviews with Christian media, weathered by constant attempts to place the band in or out of the evangelical box. "Someone asked me if I was a Christian. I don't know," Stapp concedes. "I still have a lot of questions that I wish I had answers for. I know that I believe in God and I speak with Him every day, and I have a relationship with Him and I feel like he speaks with me, and I feel like He's instrumental in everything that I do."

The debate rages on—does public acknowledgement of sorted-out faith make one a true Christian, or does the real rub occur when God is "instrumental" in someone's actions? Meanwhile, the worship service that is a Creed concert continues to sell out along the legs of the *Weathered* tour. Stapp sweats, moans, and seeks transcendent encounters at the mic, and those who have come to worship agonize with him as the struggle for meaning continues.—*John M. De Marco*

JON FOREMAN

AGE:25
BIRTHPLACE:SAN BERNARDINO, CALIFORNIA
OCCUPATION:MUSICIAN—VOCALS AND GUITAR FOR SWITCHFOOT

Jon Foreman: seeker, husband, surfer, musician, songwriter. Those are the facts. The categories. The assumptions. The things you could find out from Google. Dig a little deeper, though, and you will find a soul living, feeling, and struggling within the same tension all of us experience when we decide to live on this Earth, yet follow the call to transcend it with our soul.

How are you being relevant? To an artist on a Christian record label, this is a loaded question. It is really asking, have you ventured out of the faith ghetto? But from Foreman's answer to this very question, it's apparent he is busy trying to live life as an artist of faith in a world that many times opts for ease over glory. "Every song that really moves me has some kind of spiritual weight to it," Foreman says. "I think most people would find themselves in that category. As far as the way you express Christianity, that is a tricky thing …" It is something Foreman will continue to struggle with—being true to his

I.AM.RELEVANT

faith and himself, while avoiding categories those around him might try to impose. "I think music is certainly a valid means of expressing my beliefs—the way I view a sunset, the way I feel a life is best lived," he says.

Switchfoot was recently called to act in a movie Jason Priestly was directing. On the set, they were asked to be in an extra shot that involved filming a music video. Foreman explains, "Obviously the way we film a music video is not the way Guns 'n' Roses might film theirs, and [the producers] wanted something more along that line, with cage dancers and that whole scene. We wanted to be salt and light and try and figure out how three Christian guys who play rock and roll fit into this—how do you stand out, how do you exemplify who Christ is when they could care less who you are?" Switchfoot decided it wasn't their scene—literally. "So we just said, 'Hey, this isn't who we are as a band, obviously we don't

JON FOREMAN

"I think music is certainly a valid means of expressing my beliefs—the way I view a sunset, the way I feel a life is best lived."

believe in it artistically or morally…' They said, 'Okay, it's your decision.' We did the parts we agreed with and respectfully walked home. A couple guys came up to us afterwards and said, 'No one ever stands up for what they believe in Hollywood; thank you for doing that.'"

As an antidote to the daily artistic/professional struggle of being a working musician, Foreman likes to surf and enjoy the beauty of God's creation: "As the sun is going down over the same water you are sitting on, and everything's gold and you see dolphins swim by … it's hard to look at all that and not believe in an omnipotent creator who knows how to create beauty." —*Daniel Miller*

I.AM.RELEVANT

TOM
CONLON

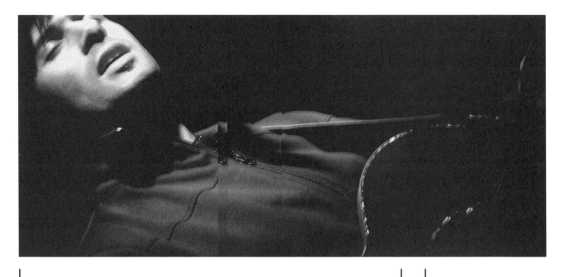

| |

AGE:33
BIRTHPLACE:BREWSTER, NEW YORK
OCCUPATION:MUSICIAN

The minute Tom Conlon enters the room, so does peace. The moment he says hello to you, you feel accepted. The second he puts a pick to his guitar and sends air through his vocal chords, you can feel angels crowd in close to hear.

Conlon is a musician who can honestly say he's not doing it to "make it big" or even to make a lot of money. His ministry, Soil Out of Sand, is about "music that is not business." Conlon travels all over the country on tour, playing his music, leading worship, and encouraging everyone he comes in contact with. He is constantly giving of his soul, his life, and his ability. Even his CDs have no set price.

It is easy to imagine that with all that giving of himself, burn-out would be an inevitability. It was. So the year 2001 was somewhat of a sabbatical for Conlon. A door opened for him to stay with friends in Boston, and he spent some time doing plumbing and heating on a 200-year-old house. "Working with my hands was very therapeutic," says Conlon. Most importantly, he played and wrote music for himself, for the sake of the art itself. Conlon puts it this way: "I grew musically in an incubating way."

With some coaxing from his inner circle, "trusting their judgment over my own," Conlon began "slowly testing the water, performing again." He found it was still something that gave him life and joy, and he decided to start touring again. He spent the first months of 2002 traveling throughout the east coast and New England, and recorded a new CD. He calls his van a "mobile record label." He has a CD burner on the passenger seat and burns his CDs as he drives from gig to gig. A friend produces the cover art. This makes Conlon a true pioneer in production-on-demand technology.

A move to his first permanent residence in five years has also entered Conlon's picture this year. He moved to New York City. "I had New York City on the brain, and felt like that was a place I could be challenged artistically and culturally," he says. He also acknowledges, "My late night schedule doesn't work well in the suburbs."

Conlon is someone who is being true to himself and his art, and in so doing he becomes an amazingly authentic person to interact with. It may just be that Conlon is living the ultimate dream: to live a true life of faith and compassion, creating beauty that not only flows from that life, but makes up that life.—*Daniel Miller*

I.AM.RELEVANT

BEBO
NORMAN

AGE:29
BIRTHPLACE:COLUMBUS, GEORGIA
OCCUPATION:SINGER/SONGWRITER

While the college years may be well behind Bebo Norman, the majority of his fans are still plugged into schools and universities across the country. It's a fan base Bebo (whose nickname comes from his little sister who couldn't pronounce "big brother") says he can still relate to and understand.

"College is such a transitional period, it's a soul-searching time in terms of trying to find your own identity in such a transient world," Norman says. "I write a lot about the questions I have, my confusions, frustrations and the things that make me happy. I think college students can relate to that because of their stage in life. And strangely enough, my world is still a lot like a college student's because of the transient nature of this career."

This self-described "Georgia boy" can mainly be found on the road performing in university towns and in front of twentysomethings who have grown older with him. Unlike many musicians whose managers hand out a limited number of backstage passes, Norman doesn't head behind the curtain after a performance. Rather, he walks straight out into the audience to talk, laugh, and share precious moments with his fans. There is a sense of community and connection he finds among the audience, and he believes wholeheartedly that it's the most important aspect of his performance.

"It can get tiring, but so can playing the same songs fifty nights in a row," he says. "Sometimes it's hard to have a million relationships that are only five minutes long. When you add it up, they can dominate your time so much when you get home with people you love, you can be so worn out relationally that those relationships suffer. I feel like now I'm in a good place where I can really balance the more temporal relationships with those that are deeper and more intimate."

Norman's signature attribute isn't found in his pop folk sound as much as it is in his lyrics which are both deep and profound. Sage-like observations on life, relationships, and Christ-like qualities seep into his work and stir a wondering in listeners' hearts and minds. But such a gifting doesn't come without cost in the record business. Norman admits he often feels a burden to be profound. "It's such a strange concept—trying to be profound—because most of the time I feel so completely un-profound. When I start thinking that way, I don't write a thing," he says. "The things that make the most sense to me in the long run just seem to kind of pop out; they don't often come from sitting down to try to see things from some different perspective. The better things seem to come out of emotion. And it takes living life to come up with those things rather than just sitting down to hole yourself up in a room somewhere." —*Margaret Feinberg*

I.AM.RELEVANT

SARA
GROVES

AGE:29
BIRTHPLACE:VINELAND, NEW JERSEY
OCCUPATION:MUSICIAN

An honest apologist through music, Sara Groves writes songs that communicate the difficulties we have keeping faith and sharing that faith with a sometimes suspicious world. In a world where confessionalism is venerated, Christians can't talk about what's at the center of their hearts without provoking. Groves has found a way to break down these barriers, and it's a surprisingly simple one: telling the truth about herself and her life through music.

Take, for example, these lyrics from "Conversations," the title track from her 2001 album:

"We've had every conversation in the world about what is right and what has all gone bad/but have I mentioned to you that this is all that I am/this is all that I have?/I would like to share with you what makes me complete/The only thing that isn't meaningless to me is Jesus Christ and the way He set me free."

Groves started her career as a singer/songwriter almost by accident. A high school English and history teacher, she played a Fellowship of Christian Athletes event, after which students began asking for recordings of her work. Soon courted by Christian record labels, she felt God was telling her to remain on her own, and released an independent album before signing with In Not Of Records.

Groves describes the new album as "very relational," keeping with her reputation for writing realistic songs about how we deal with each other and with God. Though the music industry is "in the middle of a worship phenomenon," she doesn't write worship songs. "My album picks up after the worship service is over, (and asks) how is that time with the Lord seeping into your real life situations?"

Though she plays to mostly Christian audiences now, the material that Groves writes reaches out in other ways than performing to "secular" crowds. "I have friends who felt compelled to go play bars and stuff, and I started wondering if I needed to book more non-Christian events." But, Groves says, she's never "been in a bar anyway," so why start now?

Instead, Groves says she's "providing a conversation piece for believers and nonbelievers alike to gather around the table and talk about issues that affect all of mankind, but from a Christian worldview." She also feels it's important to write songs that address the questions and doubts that are an essential part of the struggle for faith. "A radio person once asked me why I write doubting songs. I don't think I write doubting songs, I write process songs. A lot of Christian music is at point B already. I write about how you get from point A to point B. Most people are at point A."

While Groves acknowledges, "You need point B songs, where you just throw your head back and say, 'Praise the Lord,'" she's never fully arrived at that elusive point B. "'Til the Lord comes, I've never arrived."—*Jenny S. Johnson*

REESE
ROPER

AGE:28
BIRTHPLACE:STEAMBOAT SPRINGS, COLORADO
OCCUPATION:SINGER/SONGWRITER, PASTOR, SCIENTIST

Seven years is a long time for any band to be together, but Five Iron Frenzy has managed to hold it together. Lead singer Reese Roper credits the strong friendship and humility among its members. "We support each other in everything we do," he says. "I haven't seen the closeness that our band has in very many other bands. Another reason I think we have kept going so long is the fact we live in Denver as opposed to California or Nashville. It kind of separates us from all the industry stuff and fame other bands deal with. When we get home, we are treated just like everyone else. There is always this thought of having to go back to the real world when a tour is over. It is both humbling and sobering."

Five Iron Frenzy began in April 1995 as a side project of an industrial band Reese Roper and three cohorts. While they started out playing in Christian venues, it wasn't long until the group was asked to open for secular bands in local clubs and bars. "We started a Bible study to minister to the people we were talking to in the club scene," Roper recalls.

"And our church kind of grew out of that Bible study in February of 2000."

That less-than-traditional church is called Scum of the Earth, and if you visit Scum's services on Sunday night, you'll see about 100 people, many of them pierced, tattooed and enjoying alternative hair styles, stuffed into a coffee house. Pews have been replaced by couches, and after worship there's a break for hot wings and pizza. The service picks back up with a message from Roper or pastor Mike Sares, and afterward the church becomes a kind of house party.

While Scum provides a solid ministry platform for the band, Roper says it's still hard to reach people. "For us, it seems like our biggest struggle has always been trying to get people to look past us, to see the love of God, and not the rock star glitz and glamour," he says. "We have always tried to be honest and transparent. I just hate the feeling I get when people are more excited about our stupid band than they are about God."

Roper, who describes himself as a "braniac-nerd-type kid who only listened to classical music in junior high," says it seems like every time you can convince one fan that you are a normal person, there are fifty more to take their place. "It's kind of disheartening," he says. "Personally, I have been growing in patience because of this, and just how hard touring can be."

Even with the band's success and church plant, Roper says he actually wants to be a movie director. "Don't laugh!" he says. "I'm starting my own film company. I want to try and make some videos for Five Iron and our side project Brave Saint Saturn, and then move on to trying to make a feature length film. I hope it works." —*Margaret Feinberg*

I.AM.RELEVANT

DAMIEN JURADO

AGE:29
BIRTHPLACE:LOS ANGELES, CALIFORNIA
OCCUPATION:SINGER/SONGWRITER

With the reluctance of Jonah, Seattle singer/songwriter Damien Jurado accepts that his role as a musician is going to lead some fans to approach him for answers to life's biggest questions. For someone who considers faith a very personal matter, it's difficult for him to play the role of psychiatrist, counselor and pastor.

A man recently emailed him saying he had planned on committing suicide and Jurado's music helped him get through a rough time. Another fan emailed about his impending divorce. "Stuff like that happens all the time," he said. "I don't really want to get involved, but I'm glad my music can do that. I think because I'm so honest with my lyrics, they feel like they can be honest with me."

Jurado wasn't really looking for the spotlight. He was a last-minute opening act for a friend when representatives from Seattle's Subpop Records were in the audience. After the show, they asked him for a demo. He's since released four CDs on Subpop, as well as two CDs on the Made in Mexico label, including *Postcards and Audio Letters*, an unusual collection of discarded home-made audio recordings that he gathered from thrift stores.

The project got its start when Jurado was shop-

I.AM.RELEVANT

ping for cassettes. He picked up a case only to find the tape missing. In its place was a blank cassette that read, "Christmas 1980." He popped It in his Walkman and found a recording of people opening Christmas gifts. "It really just blew my mind," he said. "It became an addiction. I try to go out and find as much stuff as I can. Estate sales are big out here. People die and just leave crap in the house. You go in there and you can rummage through their things. Each one is different, but there's a common thread you often hear on these tapes—joy, sadness, anger—a little reminder how human we are and how fragile life is. There's a certain sadness to it that these people's lives and emotions end up in a thrift store for ten cents."

The project has gotten national media attention, and Jurado has a follow-up CD in the works, this time with his own music in the background. The audio letters have also served as inspiration for his own songwriting. "I just try to be honest," he said. "I try to write songs about real things. That way people can relate to them. I don't talk about the spiritual aspect as much. If I do talk about heaven or God, it's more as a question."—*Josh Jackson*

JENNIFER KNAPP

AGE:28
BIRTHPLACE:CHANUTE, KANSAS
OCCUPATION:SINGER/SONGWRITER

It takes a while for most musicians to get noticed, but Jennifer Knapp didn't have to wait long. In 1999, she won the Dove Award for Best New Artist. Since then, she's received widespread applause both in and out of Christian circles. *The Los Angeles Times*, *Pollstar Magazine* and *People Magazine* have been singing her praises, and *Billboard* says, "Knapp proves herself to be the cream that rises to the top."

Despite such loud overtures, Knapp still describes herself as the "girl with a guitar." But don't let the rootsy Kansas-born singer-songwriter fool you; she has sold nearly a million albums. Unlike many who stumble upon such success, Knapp still carries a rugged, natural appeal. Rather than toting the "right" answer, as most polished stars become accustomed to delivering, Knapp still prefers more off-the-cuff, honest and sometimes even witty, sarcastic replies. The mantra "just be yourself" isn't something Knapp preaches, it's something she lives.

"I'm kind of like a shy person," Knapp confesses. "But when I'm working, it's kind of differ-ent. I think over the last seven years that I've been involved on stage I've grown in that confidence just as I've grown into being an adult and in my faith. I became a Christian at eighteen and within two years was on stage. When you write a Christian song, then you have to be Christian leader, which is bizarre. I've had to learn that and had to become passionate about some things along the way. If I'm confident in a subject then I'm more prone to be confident about it as a person."

While the folk-inspired rock artist may feel "chicken" when no one is looking, she isn't afraid to write about her struggles, weaknesses, and failings, which makes her human, and more importantly, accessible to her fans.

"As I've gotten further into the Jesus role model, there are certain times I'm thinking and writing and forget about everything else, and then I move into the mind frame, 'How can I say this so as to not get the backlash of community I live in and at the same time discuss a struggle that no one else is talking about?'

.MORE ❯

I.AM.RELEVANT

JENNIFER KNAPP

"I want to be able to talk about things that are important and relevant.
I'm not [always] Christ-like, but that's still the goal."

"As time has gone on, it's been a personal struggle. I want to be able to talk about things that are important and relevant. I'm not [always] Christ-like, but that's still the goal. That's a catch-22 in this environment. I've had to struggle more to hold onto vulnerability. People who want it are screaming for it. So you've got two sides: the people who are demanding to hear your life story, and other people who say, 'Shut up, that's not right, your real isn't real.'"

Even in the midst of struggling with her identity as an individual, believer, and performer, Knapp has been showered with comparisons of artists such as Natalie Merchant, Sheryl Crow, and Tracy Chapman. The twenty-eight-year-old musician says that while such comparisons "freaked [her] out," she's grown to a place where she's comfortable just being Jennifer Knapp. —*Margaret Feinberg*

I.AM.RELEVANT

FLYNN ADAM ATKINS

AGE:29
BIRTHPLACE:HUNTINGBIRD, INDIANA
OCCUPATION:RAPPER, PRODUCER

Try this for a resume. Flynn Atkins, one-eighth of left-coast hip-hop act LA Symphony, has two solo records housed under his own label, Eartube Empire, not to mention his crew's much talked about debut, *Call It What You Want*, which is poised to infect the mainstream. He's in the process of writing a book about dating and producing a short film on the Los Angeles social structure. And let's face it: He's a successful white emcee from Middle America. Period. But what does the Vanguard University English/film-making graduate consider his finest achievement? "I'm actually following my dreams," he says. "Everyone has ideas of succeeding and doing something different, it's just whether or not they put their walk where their talk is."

For the Indiana native, those dreams of thriving in hip-hop culture came to fruition after hooking up with partner in crime Pigeon John at a wedding more than a decade ago—a collaboration that would result in late-night production sessions at the school Communications lab and ultimately the formation of rap powerhouse LA Symphony. "He really encouraged me," Flynn recalls. "He heard my raps and said that I had to get moving and do this.

"That's one of the key things as an artist and an individual, just working, making a dent in society and culture," he says. "Nothing's gonna come to you; you have to make it happen. The violent really do take by force." He then tags, "I'm not saying you have to be forceful. But you can't sit on your rump and not do anything."

Flynn's been off that rump for a while, giving music audiences, especially the Christian sector, a crash course on underground hip-hop music. It all stems from a lack of talent he perceives in the industry. "We like to call it 'crap,'" he lightheartedly responds in reference to Christian rap music. "Over the past fifteen years, the caliber and quality of that music has been so under-par that it bears negative connotations."

In fact, when it comes to Christian rap, Flynn shies away from associating his music with the genre. "For us, we say we are hip-hop artists and Christians." It's a suggestion that readily raises eyebrows in the Christian community. "A lot of people automatically deduce 'Oh, he's ashamed of the Gospel,'" he says. "I think there's an element of tact, couth, and respect that we as Christians have to exemplify to the world. Otherwise we come off looking like narrow-minded individuals who don't care about people, just about numbers and conversions, and it becomes more propaganda than heartfelt expression of faith and love." Flynn even accounts for non-Christian rappers who have already been performing at this level. "I loved Tribe Called Quest and De La Soul; they weren't pushing their beliefs onto me. Once you studied them you found out what their religious beliefs are.

"When Christ was most aggressive and no-holds barred it was with the church, Jews, and Pharisees, not the non-believers. I just think that if you are a Christian your love will be your testimony. That's how Christ was."—*Bobby Kim*

IRA
LIPPKE

AGE:27
BIRTHPLACE:DENVER, COLORADO
OCCUPATION:PHOTOGRAPHER

Ira Lippke says his art discovers and displays reality. "When we look at the world and see harmony, beauty, and meaning, it's really a discovery of God's mind," he says. A professional photographer specializing in fashion and fine art, Lippke rejects the "postmodern, relativist position that the artist is actually defining reality."

"I take more of a classical view," he says. "When I'm doing my art, I'm not creating out of nothing, I'm relaying what I see." What Lippke sees, and how he sees it, is influenced by an early conversion and unconventional upbringing. "My parents were hippies; we grew up moving around," he says. The family attended the Science of the Mind Church until "God totally saved my family, with barely any outside influence," Lippke says. After a Rainbow Gathering in Washington state, the family and their caravan stopped at a cherry orchard to work. Ira rode his bike into town and happened to encounter a vacation Bible school in the park where the seven year old met Christ. "I went back and told my family I was a Christian and they were, like, 'Cool, we all are,'" he says. Later, their van broke down in the Olympic rain forest with no money for gas. "We were living in a tent, and my parents took my Bible and read the gospels, and it was just undeniable to them, Jesus' character and teaching. Our family devoted our lives to the Lord there in the Olympic rainforest."

From the rainforest, Ira eventually discovered photography, entered Biola University as the first home-schooled student receiving its highest academic scholarship, and started his career as a photographer. These days he also runs the Labrys Contemporary Art Gallery, which is hosted by Lippke's Church, Long Beach Grace Brethren.

"Christians are very concerned about what's happening with our culture, but Christians have been pulling out of it, or segregating and making a separate culture that doesn't impact the culture we're living in." Furthermore, he says, "it's embarrassing when things are done in poor quality. Specifically, if you're called to be involved in culture, you're called to do it really really well and with integrity. If more Christians would merely do that, our culture would be transformed."

Lippke tries to do that as a fashion photographer. "On a shoot, you spend a lot of time hanging out, and topics of faith come up all the time," he says. "Today, people are really open to spirituality. When they see an authentic spirituality, they're receptive to it. I think I've broken some stereotypes of what a Christian looks like, and enabled people to see that I can serve God and do what I feel I need to be doing."

Indeed, Lippke says there's no contradiction between his Christian convictions and work in fashion. "Many people think it isn't possible to serve God and work in the fashion industry at the same time," he says. "It's God's plan that we wear clothes, that we express ourselves and try to do things beautifully. It's a delight in the art of creating beauty and self-expression."—*Jenny S. Johnson*

I.AM.RELEVANT

JASON MARTIN

AGE:29
BIRTHPLACE:LOS ANGELES, CALIFORNIA
OCCUPATION:MUSICIAN

Tooth and Nail Records' most veteran group, Starflyer 59, has cranked out more than a dozen full-length projects across the past nine years. And while music remains only a part-time job for lead singer Jason Martin, he cannot imagine any other vocational passion in life.

Martin joined the music scene at age fourteen when his older brother Ronnie (a member of Joy Electric) started a band and let Jason participate. The younger Martin began playing guitar around age sixteen and tried to write some songs. Martin says his lyrics are "a lot about life, and what's going on with [him] and [his] family." "We're not extremely evangelical in my lyrics. I hope my faith comes through with them. I have a weird thing about putting the Lord's name in everything—I feel like it could be taken in vain just to throw it in casually because it rhymes with something."

Martin, who has two small children and works full-time for his family's trucking company, says the band sees its purpose as creating quality entertainment. "We're just trying to be legit. We're not trying to be the Christian version of this or that band. I'm not out to hide the fact I believe in Christ. Christian or otherwise, our goal is to put out good music. To the glory of God we should do the best we can do," he says.

Starflyer frequent plenty of clubs—embracing line-ups that are pretty evenly balanced between Christian and mainstream venues—connecting with lots of young music fans but not overtly seeking to engineer conversions of faith. Playing the club scene and working his day job afford Martin plenty of opportunities to mix with unchurched individuals. The truck delivery gig doesn't allow many extended conversations, but Martin notes that a few opportunities for faith-sharing have popped up during the years. "I've probably missed about twenty opportunities, in that I'm a sinful guy and don't always speak when I should," he admits.

Martin and Starflyer have enjoyed their relationship with Seattle-based Tooth and Nail, Christian music's leading label for hard and alternative types of rock music. "It's a cool situation. We can do the record we want to do, and not hear any kind of moaning because certain songs are eight minutes or whatever. We don't have some guy on our back telling me to change everything we've been working on."

Looking to the future, Martin says his only clear plans are to keep cutting more music. "It's hard to say—five years ago I wouldn't have thought I'd still be pulling out records. Maybe some day I can make a living at doing this."—*John M. De Marco*

TONÉX

AGE:26
BIRTHPLACE:SAN DIEGO, CALIFORNIA
OCCUPATION:RECORDING ARTIST

Since the age of thirteen, Tonex knew he was called to ministry but also realized he couldn't fit into a stuffy church mold. The young preacher/musician developed his own look and musical style expressed on his coming-of-age independent album, *Silent 'X' 516*, which was recorded on the same low-key indie label that originally recorded P.O.D. His follow-up release, *Damage*, was only released on cassette because of limited funds.

The stalwart eighteen year old would sell the cassettes out of the trunk of his car in front of stores, including mass merchants Wal-Mart and K-Mart. "I would have tables outside car washes and people who knew me would just laugh," he recalls. "I was determined, though. I didn't care what people thought. I told them that in a couple of years, everyone will know who I am."

Two years later, the self-prophecy came into fruition when *Pronounced Toe-Nay* dropped. Although it was an independent album, word of mouth spread like wildfire and soon five labels ended up fighting for the record. Three years later, the agonizing battle was won by Jive/Verity and *Pronounced Toe-Nay* was re-released with two less songs. "The issues I addressed on the album were issues that were not addressed in Christian music before, in such a bold way, and people really connected with it," Tonex says. "Most Christian gospel albums tell of perfect Christians who pray every day and live perfect lives, but I don't have a choir popping out of my closet in the morning for breakfast. The album was about me not allowing religion to dictate what I wanted to be."

Tonex's 2002 release, *02*, is described as more bright, beautiful, colorful, and optimistic. "I'm a lot more focused now," Tonex says. "Marriage has brought a lot of maturation to me." Yvette (Graham) Williams, Tonex's wife, was the lead singer on three of the Grammy-winning Thompson Community Singers' albums, and now plans to release her own solo album. The song "You" on Tonex's *02* release tells their love story. "Yvette is such a supportive

.MORE   ❯

I.AM.RELEVANT

TONEX

"The album was about me not allowing religion to dictate what I wanted to be."

wife," Tonex says admiringly. "She sings background for me on the road and says to me, 'It's not about me right now. You do what you have to do.' It's amazing to see someone who is so talented but unselfish."

Reflecting on his musical and spiritual journey, Tonex believes originality is the key. "The Lord wants to use our uniqueness for His glory and [it's easy to] feel you have to emulate a lot to fit the status quo, but it's those who go against the grain that become the trail blazers. Initially, people are afraid of it and it is rejected, but when it's from God, it will become a trend, and I know God wants us to be trendsetters and not trend followers."
—*Margaret Feinberg*

I.AM.RELEVANT

RON IRIZARRY

AGE:29
BIRTHPLACE:CARLISLE, PENNSYLVANIA
OCCUPATION:SINGER/SONGWRITER

If you've taken in a show from the likes of 'NSync, Jordan Knight, Pink, Sisqo, or Mandy Moore during the past few years, you might recall an opening act featuring a dark-haired guy with sunglasses and a really positive way about him.

Ron Irizarry sports a dream catcher tattoo on the left side of his waist, a sun around his navel and a Celtic cross on his right shoulder blade. He digs rock climbing and loves to drink Lambic Frambiose. His favorite film is *The Shawshank Redemption* and his favorite book is the Bible. And through his musical talents of singing and playing the guitar and violin, he's connected with both mainstream audiences and the Christian pop culture.

Growing up, music was a staple in the Irizarry home. "Dad had an organ and Mom had a voice, so there would always be music," Irizarry says. The violin was chosen for him, but when he hit his teen years, Irizarry wanted "a hipper instrument." Dad came home with an electric guitar. Irizarry's been clutching one ever since.

Irizarry hooked up with 'NSync founder Chris Kirkpatrick when both were college students in central Florida. They went their separate ways after college, with Irizarry playing guitar for several Christian music industry artists and Kirkpatrick moving on to stardom in the late 1990s with his boy band. The pair re-connected, and in 1999 Irizarry found himself on tour.

These days, Irizarry spends most of his time hopping across the country and playing at college campuses. "It's me and my acoustic guitar," he says. "I'm kind of going back to the basics. It's like a coffee shop atmosphere. That's what I've always loved." The campus tour stops afford plenty of opportunities for Irizarry to chill with students. "I love hanging out with college people. You get to know them, to build relationships."

Irizarry meets them where they are, and many permit him the same courtesy. "I think the word 'Christian' has been given a bad name by a lot of different people," Irizarry says. "What I find is that as soon as you bring that up, people turn off. I just live my life. I had a bunch of guys ask me what kind of music I played—they said there's something different about it."

Something different. Something that stands out and makes you think. Most of Irizarry's songs are relationship-oriented. Here and there, amid the lyrics, you can find questions about life and spiritual experiences. It's the output of a regular guy writing and singing about what he sees and hears and feels. It's a natural outflow of a heart that is curious and adventurous. And there's no specific game plan in Irizarry's life other than to embrace the journey. "My work ethic is to always keep moving, always keep going forward," he says. "I know God put everyone on earth for a reason. I seek His will and kind of go along as I hear it."—*John M. De Marco*

I.AM.RELEVANT

NICK
PURDY

AGE:30
BIRTHPLACE:FT. GORDON, GEORGIA
OCCUPATION:MEDIA ENTREPRENEUR

Nick Purdy grew up in the Bible Belt, became a Christian relatively young, and worked in Christian ministry with Campus Crusade for Christ after graduating college. So friends and family were a little surprised when he decided to pull up his Southern roots and move to Seattle with no specific job opportunity in mind. "My wife and I had a growing sense of unease living in metro Atlanta," he says. "We looked up one day and noticed that we hardly knew any non-Christians. We perceived that to be a problem and were worried if we didn't get out of that lifestyle, that over time we'd lose the ability to effectively relate to non-believers. Being neck-deep in cultural Christianity was killing me."

They decided to pick somewhere completely different, and a good friend had just left to start a church in urban Seattle. Purdy was both challenged and liberated as he was part of a church plant in this new environment. "What was surprising," he says, "was that as far as non-Christians, God put people in our lives who had really been burned by religion and had a very negative experience with it and assumed that the church really wasn't a place for them.

"For us, living out Christianity in a culture like Seattle was a lot different because, in the South, there was a sense we were supposed to look like we had everything together. In Seattle, it was more honest and real and way more effective to be quite frank about our pathos or 'screwed-up-ness.' So that actually led us into more relationships with non-believers and people that had been involved in the church but had some antagonism towards it."

Purdy juggled his church duties and a job with a local marketing firm with his true passion—PasteMusic.com, a website aimed at helping artists market and sell their own music. While his fledgling company slowly grew, he spent a valuable and profitable year as an e-business consultant at Deloitte & Touche. With the end of the dot-com era and the church well-established, the Purdys decided it was time to move back closer to family and his PasteMusic business partners.

He's now able to spend much of his time listening to new songwriters and bands and grow his business. While many of the artists he works with are Christians who have targeted a broader audience, many simply play music that seems to search for deeper, more meaningful truths.

"One thing that has frustrated me over the years is in a very real way, there's this false divide between the sacred and the secular. For the Christian, anything that you do that's not sin can and should be worship. So as we encounter art that's just good, that makes the world a better place, that reflects some degree of truth, we feel like that's the type of music to put our brand name behind and help promote. We hope that the stuff that we put out is a sort of gospel leaven in the cultural loaf."—*Josh Jackson*

MG!
THE VISIONARY

AGE:TWENTYSOMETHING
BIRTHPLACE:SEATTLE, WASHINGTON
OCCUPATION:RAPPER

Right out of high school, Martin Brazier Jr.—dubbed MG! The Visionary
(as in Man of God with a vision to be as highly influential and visible as possible and
make an impact on the world)—began pursuing a music career. "Music was all around
me when I was coming to know the Lord," says the hip-hop artist. "We were sick of the
cheesy Christian rap and since the stuff on the radio had bangin' beats but horrible messages, we just decided to do our own thing."

MG! says he never got caught up in trying to land a record deal. Instead, he focused on
doing what he loved to do and that, in turn, created a huge buzz. He cut five independent albums before being approached by Brandon Ebel to be a founding member of a
new hip-hop division for Tooth and Nail Records. MG!, along with his team, actually
came up with the name—Uprok Records—and designed the label's unique logo. "I've
had freedom to run," he says. "I do all my own production from the ground up in my studio, the Reign Room. Every release I've put out has been the same way and I do not

intend to change that, risking the loss of creative control or the spirit I desire to capture in my music.

"On average you hear a rapper sing sort of about himself and what he does or has and whatnot. As a generalization, you don't feel like you know him better by the end of the song ... in essence you relate more to the music and rhythm then you do with the artist. With rock, you hear this guy talking about his life pouring his soul out over melodies and emotional harmonies, like Creed, and you feel like you know that person a little more by the end of the song ... like you can relate to him, and that's the main connection. I'm trying to bring the two things together.

"I think that is an element we lack in most mainstream hip-hop," he says. "It's the biggest music in the world, but along with that the images aren't what I feel we need as portrayed on pop television or radio. I want to bring heart and soul back into the hip-hop music. I cannot imagine a career as fun or rewarding as making music, but we also need to be responsible with it."

The hip-hop artist headed in a new direction with his second recording from Uprock. *Sinner's Prayer Vol. 1—Declaring War* is described by MG! as the "first full-length praise and worship hip-hop album on earth."

"When you think of praise and worship, a certain image comes to mind," he says. "Sometimes praise and worship is related more to a sound or style rather than the heart of the music itself. I have a different perspective; I believe it's all about the heart."— *Margaret Feinberg*

I.AM.RELEVANT

CLAIRE HOLLEY

AGE:30
BIRTHPLACE:JACKSON, MISSISSIPPI
OCCUPATION:SINGER/SONGWRITER

For Claire Holley, the biggest temptation she faces playing music on the bar circuit is not one of the typical rock star vices like sex or drugs. It's believing the performer is the most important person in the room. "Living out Christianity on a daily basis is challenge enough," she says, "but being in the music business doesn't make it any easier. It's hard to stay humble in a profession where so much time is devoted to promoting yourself. Even songwriting—as much as I love it and need it—can feed the self-absorption."

Holley released her third CD, a self-titled album on Yep Roc Records last year, and her music was recently featured on NPR. As her career progressed, she realized that she needed to find ways to keep herself grounded. Last year, she began volunteering weekly at a local hospice. "When you sing songs to people who are dying and might not live to the next day," she says, "it makes the songs more immediate. And it makes you think about your life differently. I felt that I had a lot to be grateful for. I'm alive, and I got to sing for these people, and I love that."

Though her second CD, *Sanctuary*, was a collection of hymns, Holley has always felt more comfortable working outside the Christian music industry. Her faith comes through in her music without being heavy-handed, and she's able to convey truths to people who might not be open to hearing them otherwise.

While her songs are filled with a Christian perspective on subjects like life and death, love and hate, faith and doubt, and God, they have been well-received by a broad spectrum of listeners. Ironically, when her label explored the idea of marketing her music in Christian bookstores, the content of a couple of songs closed those doors. That was simply a confirmation for her that she'd chosen the right path.

"I really enjoy the label I'm working with," she says. "I'm a pretty quirky person. I've done a CD with hymns, and I've done a couple of CDs with a band, and I'm thinking of working on music for films. I feel like in some ways Yep Roc has done a better job of letting me be who I need to be—which happens to be a Christian—better than a Christian label would."

So Holley will continue writing her songs, sharing them with people and finding joy in the simpler things like serving others. "I imagine that most artists would say that it's easier to write a song about a down-and-out person rather than to spend an afternoon with him. Both are needed and important. Learning to live within that tension is, for me, at the heart of being a Christian and an artist."—*Josh Jackson*

I.AM.RELEVANT

BEN PASLEY

AGE:THIRTYSOMETHING
BIRTHPLACE:MILLBROOK, ALABAMA
OCCUPATION:WRITER, MUSICIAN, CHURCH BUILDER

Ben Pasley believes the future of the church will be worked out in a pub over beers. Or thereabouts. His conviction is based not on a belief in the centrality of alcohol, but in the importance of personal relationships to the perpetuation of Christ's community.

Known for his and wife Robin's group 100 Portraits and the book *Enter the Worship Circle* (Relevant Books), Pasley is also "obsessed with sharing Christ with young people who have no experience in the traditional church," he says. "They're meeting a new dynamic—Jesus—who they're willing to embrace, but the traditional church is like a cultural airplane ticket to another country for them. It's messed up my life, because I'm no longer satisfied with just being an artist or evangelist. I desperately want to see young people won into the family, so I have to be part of creating the family."

Pasley's strategy eschews traditional concepts of the church, which he says places too much importance on buildings and facilities. "Culture is so desperate to understand Christ, and they know He died for the church, but what they don't understand is why He died for a building," he says. "The Bible says forsake not the assembly of yourselves together, which I think means not to forsake the challenge to aggressively pursue committed relationships. Aggressively pursuing being in the same room does not build relationships."

Building relationships is what Pasley's doing with Blue Renaissance, a mentoring organization for young Christian artists. Blue Renaissance also models the relational concept of church. Since members' callings keep them traveling, they can't attach to a particular local body. Instead, they attach to each other and non-Christians within their sphere of influence. Blue Renaissance played host to Blue Door, an interactive art project installed in a local theater, where Christians and pre-Christians (Pasley's term) could share art, get to know one another and, perhaps later, go for a beer. On the basis of Blue Door's artistic strengths, relationships were forged with non-Christians, including an owner of a local vinyl record store and theater director.

Pasley says it's no accident so many young Christians are finding their callings in ministry through the arts. "One reason for this intense renewal in the arts is that God loves looking for the lost coins in the couch cushions," he says. "Our culture has become more emotional, less rational, more romantic, where the transfer of language and truth is better achieved by the arts than academic forms. If that's true, and the Lord loves people, He'll adjust his language to reach them. He's called the artist to an extremely high level of responsibility, maybe higher than we know."

Those looking for clues to Pasley's future artistic direction have surprises in store. His current music is influenced by ethnic fusion, a passion fueled by annual trips to India. But beyond that, he says, "I have a very specific plan. Deep in me there's some Alabama fatback rock 'n' roll music. It's almost a lost art form. That stuff brews in me." You heard it here first.—*Jenny S. Johnson*

MINISTRY
SECTION.THREE

MIKE MCBRIDE

AGE:28
BIRTHPLACE:ST. JOSEPH'S, MICHIGAN
OCCUPATION:BUSINESS CONSULTANT, VOLUNTEER COACH

Mike McBride spends any given work week in cities across the country, helping manufacturing companies implement new software and make their operations more efficient. But every weekend during basketball season, you can find him driving around the run-down neighborhoods of Atlanta's Techwood Community, looking for his players.

The last four years, the young business consultant has volunteered to coach in a local urban basketball league run by the Atlanta Youth Project. Since none of the fifteen to eighteen year olds he coaches have their own cars and most can't afford public transportation every week, McBride picks them up and drops them off for games on Saturday and practice on Sunday. "It's not always readily apparent where they're going to be," he says with a laugh. "So I'm often driving around trying to find them wherever their friends tell me they usually hang out."

McBride first came to Atlanta with a campus ministry, the Navigators, during the spring break of 1994, when he was attending the Purdue University. He helped clean up an old gym and build some walls and a locker room in an impoverished area of the city for the Atlanta Youth Project. After college, he took a job in Atlanta, but didn't think much about getting involved in urban ministry again until some college friends encouraged him to see what he might be able to do. He found out the Atlanta Youth Project organized a basketball league that offered kids a chance to participate in organized sports and get exposed to the Gospel. In January of 1998, he contacted Kenny Cash, who had been coaching two teams in the Techwood area. Cash wanted to concentrate his efforts on the middle school kids, so McBride took over the high school team. It hasn't been without its challenges. "I only have influence on them twice a week at practice and game times," he says. "I'm inheriting whoever they are. They come as a product of their family upbringing, their schools, their faith, their basic human sinful nature. Some of the kids are not exactly subordinate to authority."

In his first year, one such player proved to be the biggest challenge. He was one of the best players on the team, but always had to have the ball. "If the rest of the team wasn't playing how he wanted to, he would just sit on the court," McBride says. "One game in a tournament, he just got fed up with it, and sat down at the end of the court. It's not exactly obvious how you handle that."

McBride has learned during the last four years that discipline and encouragement are two of his best tools in reaching out to these kids. He brings down other volunteers and watches how much simply spending time with his players and sharing his Christian faith with them has an impact. —*Josh Jackson*

I.AM.RELEVANT

TOM SLATER

AGE:33
BIRTHPLACE:SAN JOSE, CALIFORNIA
OCCUPATION:ROCK-CLIMBING EXPERT, SURFER, TEACHER

"Slater—up here!" Students shout from every level of the bleachers. Scruffy freshmen plead for their eighth grade English teacher to join them for the rowdy fun and popularity contest of "who's sitting with who" at Friday night's Homecoming game.

Not every junior high teacher can say he has students lining up to hang out with him after the semester is over. But not every junior high teacher makes kids feel this cool, either. Whether he's inviting the loner into his classroom for lunch or the on-the-edge rebel out with him to surf, this thirty-three year old is known for having best friends who aren't old enough to drive themselves home.

Tom Slater is the older brother you've always wanted. He'll take you rock-climbing in Pinnacles National Monument on routes he created himself, motorboat you out to a private surf spot in Santa Barbara, and lead you through the back country of Yosemite—and that's just the first week of summer vacation.

Known for always embarking on new adventures with young friends, Slater may just seem like fun and games. But his students know him as the teacher and friend who challenge them to think about the larger picture in life. "A lot of people

I.AM.RELEVANT

think that in public schools, you can't talk about God. But I can leave windows open in discussion so Christian students can talk about their faith," he explains. "Or if we discuss how people from different backgrounds might view a metaphor in a book, I'm able to present the Christian viewpoint as another valid option."

One year, he traveled with twelve former students to Mexico City. "On Easter morning, I was able to whip out my Bible and read them the story of the resurrection. At sunrise, sitting outside in an ancient land with so much history, the story was very stirring, even for students who had never been to church."

Using the classroom as a starting point to form solid friendships, Slater continues to invest in his students years after they graduate. "When one of my students started high school, his parents split up and he started experimenting with alcohol. He was able to come to me for help because he knew I wouldn't flip out." Later that year, Slater invited that same student on a surf trip to Costa Rica where the two of them were able to spend more time talking and praying. "Every morning, we'd kneel in the sand to pray before we hit the waves. We went with two other people who both have a strong, visible faith and I think that kind of meaningful time with other Christians was what he needed. Now he's in college and we still get together to surf, pray, and talk whenever he comes home on break."

Whether he's surfing, rock-climbing, or teaching, Slater continues to show kids there's something beyond the every day struggles and ultimately, something in life to stay passionate about. —*Jennifer Ashley*

REBECCA MAHER

AGE:26
BIRTHPLACE:TARLBORO, NORTH CAROLINA
OCCUPATION:ADMINISTRATIVE ASSISTANT, VOLUNTEER

While Rebekah Maher spends her days working at a mortgage company, her heart is elsewhere—with children. Always eager to hold infants and nurture young ones, she began serving children in her father's church at an early age. Sunday School classes and Vacation Bible School quickly became her passion. In Maher's teen years, she began working at local preschools as an assistant caregiver.

In 1997, Maher began working at the Space Coast Early Intervention Center in Melbourne, Florida, where she jumped into the arena of children with disabilities. The program, which helps mainstream disabled children into regular elementary school, has an extremely high success rate, and Maher found her job very rewarding.

She felt led to move to Kansas City in 2000 and spend a year working and serving as part of the International House of Prayer (IHOP), but she couldn't deny her desire to work with young ones. She quickly joined a mentoring program where she worked with seventh grade inner city kids. "I'd target the trouble makers, because I knew they were also the ones with the greatest potential for leadership," she says. "I loved it."

A year later, Maher transitioned from direct ministry into the workplace at a local mortgage company. In the spring of 2001, she began working with terminally sick and dying kids at Children's Mercy Hospital in Kansas City, Missouri. Every Monday night, she and a group of volunteers have "Tuck-in-Time" with the children.

"We read stories to the children one-on-one in their hospital rooms," she explains. "As we read to the children, we try to show them the love of God in every way we can. Our heart is also to bring comfort, peace, and love to the families of the children who have the burdens of the world upon their shoulders. To say that this time is incredibly special and precious would be a total understatement."

On Tuesday nights, she volunteers her personal time to hold babies in the hospital which frees parents to take a break, eat, and get some rest. In addition, Maher helps present a monthly "Wednesday Night Live," where volunteers find activities the children would love to do outside of the hospital and bring them to the kids.

"I live for God first, but after Him I live for these children at the hospital," she says. "I come alive when I go there at night time. My passion stirs insanely during this time. I am like an enormous mother hen with these babies and children. I love just being there with the children and if I can in any way bring laughter, hope, and life to them and their families, I feel like ... well, really there is no feeling to compare it to on earth.

"The only thing I can say is I feel extremely tapped into Heaven during this time and the Father's heart for these little ones who He holds in the palm of His hand."
—Margaret Feinberg

I.AM.RELEVANT

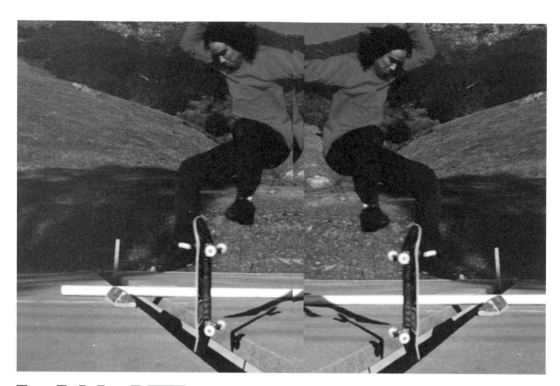

MIKE
LAW

AGE:30
BIRTHPLACE:HAWAII
OCCUPATION:ALTERNATIVE YOUTH WORKER

There was a time when Mike Law spent his hours fighting off menacing rats in Vietnam. Playing soccer in the streets of Ho Chi Mihn and turning down prostitutes as he slinked through Chinatown after dark. But mostly, during his travels after graduation, he thought about becoming an international businessman like his father.

Law had lived in a handful of countries by the age of twenty and was searching for the next step. He grew up in L.A., Hawaii, and El Salvador. Spent time in China, Thailand, and Bangkok. And after slogging through college classes in the States, the wide world awaited him. "On that trip, I was able to look at what the world of business could offer," Law says. "I kept thinking, would this be the life for me? Continue traveling, make a bunch of money?"

But the only business this ex-skategrom and punk rocker could viably get into might be distributing Red Bull and Chupa Chup lollipops. Law is quintessentially the kid who never grew up. He's always wired. Stoked on life. For a guy who just turned thirty, he blends remarkably well with people under twenty everywhere he turns. "In Ho Chi Mihn, when all I wanted to do was look for cool places to eat and hang out with random kids, I knew I had to be faithful with what God had given me."

For Law, being faithful meant not chasing after the business dreams of his parents' generation. God had clearly given him a respect for and inevitable connection with kids, however laced with mayhem they might be. After considering starting a youth ministry overseas, Law decided to return to his upper-middle class college town and continue what he did between classes, hang out with junior high kids through Young Life Ministries.

But in San Luis Obispo, a college town that gets whiter when the student population leaves on break, Law is an anomaly. He's Hawaiian, Chinese, and Filipino. He flicks around an unruly black ponytail and dresses like it's laundry day. And as a full-time youth worker who balances his time with visiting kids in juvi, driving them to drug and alcohol meetings and taking them on week-long road trips to skate parks as far as Oregon, he's surrounded by upwardly mobile suit and tie types who think he should get a real job.

"I struggle with doing ministry in a majority white town, I really do," he admits. "But, God has brought me the kids who are somewhat like me: marginalized." Law's entourage is just that: "These kids aren't white, rich, or law-abiding. The conservative churches in his town wouldn't know what to do with them."

After illegally skating some remote rooftops of the local college campus, Law admits that even skateboarding comes and goes. "As a youth worker, I can keep up with the trends in order to relate to kids, but more importantly I need to have a meaningful relationship with them and be clear about how Jesus is real in my life." —*Jennifer Ashley*

ASHLEY BERRY SELLNER

AGE:26
BIRTHPLACE:CULPEPER, VIRGINIA
OCCUPATION:PHOTOGRAPHER

Ashley Berry Sellner's interest in photography began her senior year at Wake Forest University when she decided to audit a social photography course. Upon graduation, she set her camera down and delved into her major, art history, and the pursuit of the decorative arts.

In 1998, she developed Sweet Pea: Hand-painted Furniture and Floorcloths and worked to create a successful business painting found objects, school desks, chairs, and old beds. Despite her customers' appreciation, she realized she was never quite satisfied with the product. "My passion for perfection soon led me back to photography," she says. "I love that chance moment when lighting, expression, and composition coincide to create the perfect image."

For the past year, Sellner has worked as a freelance photographer, contracted to photograph weddings for Catch Light Studio in Charlotte, North Carolina. In July 2001, she opened Sweet Pea Studio with a focus on children's portraiture and the tag line "Whimsical Portraits of Your Little Ones." She says she started the business small, doing very little marketing. Most of her customers have found out about Sweet Pea Studio through word of mouth.

Sellner says friends constantly tell her how fortunate she is to have a job that affords her time at home and allows her to do what she loves. "In my head, I'm thinking, 'If only I had the stability of your work: nine to five, consistent income, responsibilities neatly listed on a planner,'" she says. "But the truth remains, my creative spirit cannot be caged within corporate walls. I do get to live out my dreams because I am gifted with a husband who supports my passion and encourages risk taking.

"While my pocketbook is empty, my spirit is abounding in joy and excitement for what's to come," she says. "I had to knock on doors and make cold calls. I had to be willing to blindly step out of a job that was comfortable. I had to listen to my passion and not be satisfied with anything less."

Before pursuing her dream job, Sellner worked with Young Life for eight years. "It was easy to stand in the midst of a crowd of believers; now I'm learning to stand up on my own," she says. "The principles of relational evangelism transfer into the secular world perfectly. I believe a successful business comes from loyal and satisfied customers. I try to move a step beyond the relationship of photographer and client to form a more lasting friendship."

Recently Sellner did some pro bono work for a charter school sponsored by her church. She visited several elementary school classes and caught moments within their school day. The images have been used in literature, videos, and brochures. "Often people feel they are called to ministry, when in fact, they are oblivious to the opportunities around them," she says. "We need people with a heart for God everywhere—in the banking industry, in sales, in the retail market, and in our schools." —*Margaret Feinberg*

I.AM.RELEVANT

EMILY HENDEL AND MATT LANG

AGE:25
BIRTHPLACE:TOLEDO, OHIO AND OLEAN, NEW YORK
OCCUPATION:MISSIONARIES

So you've finished college and are uncertain as to what direction your vocation should take for, say, the next ten to twenty years. What to do in the meantime? Volunteer as a missionary, immersing yourself in an unfamiliar culture while touching people's lives by embracing their struggles. Such has been the choice of Emily Hendel and Matt Lang, currently finishing a second year of service with the Presbyterian Church, U.S.A., and helping dis-empowered individuals in Nashville, Tennessee.

Each previously completed a missionary stint overseas, with Hendel assisting developmentally challenged adults in Reading, England, and Lang working with human rights issues in the Philippines. "It was a year of growth for me spiritually, a year to experience a new culture, and a humbling year of building relationships with a population I hadn't been involved with ... getting to know them and all of the gifts they had to offer," says Hendel, who started dating Lang when both were students at the College of Wooster in Wooster, Ohio.

After finishing her assignment in England, Hendel began to lay the groundwork for earning a nursing degree—but still felt called to additional missionary service. The PCA then assigned her and Lang to its Nashville Epiphany Project,

I.AM.RELEVANT

which calls for the couple to divide their time between Nashville's Second Presbyterian Church and Manna, Incorporated, a non-profit hunger relief agency. "Part of our role at the church is to get involved and encourage the members of the congregation to re-examine the way they do missions themselves," Hendel says.

Hendel also works with Alternative Connections, a group for mothers who are current or past welfare recipients, seeking to effect positive changes in the welfare system. "It's encouraging to see them try to empower themselves so they can try and make a difference," she says. "They're not looked at as a group that has very much power. They're trying to educate themselves on how the system works so they can have a voice."

Lang also is working with Tying Nashville Together, organizing individuals to have more self-determination and become involved in the political process of the city. "The issue I've been working on most recently has been public schools," he says, "and the huge gap in the quality of some schools. Some have all the resources they could need; others have out of date textbooks, leaking roofs, heating that doesn't work, electrical problems. It's an issue around which we can get a lot of people mobilized."

When their service in Nashville concludes, Hendel will pursue her nursing degree, a calling she feels combines her passion for science with building relationships. Lang will attend seminary, possibly enter the ordained ministry and almost certainly will stay involved in some aspect of community organizing.

"I feel that through other people, God has shown me a lot of compassion," Hendel says. "I feel I am called to do the same thing—to show people what I know of God through getting to know them as [people] and building relationships with them." —*John M. De Marco*

MATT BRINKMANN

AGE:30
BIRTHPLACE:CEDAR RAPIDS, IOWA
OCCUPATION:PRODUCTION COMPANY OWNER, DRUMMER FOR THE CALL EVENTS

When Matt Brinkmann says to you, "Yeah, I'm a drummer in a worship band and I run my own media company, but … so what?" he's not being obnoxious or even pessimistic. He's keeping his head on straight. He means to say, What does God care if I make music or a few commercials? What God truly cares about is this: that I am in His presence and I enjoy Him—that and nothing else.

"It doesn't matter if I succeed or if I'm torn to shreds," he says. "All that matters is that I love God with all my soul and I can do that just by existing. Not by doing anything, really. Just by being."

And as this thirty year old humbly explains his faith and worth in God's eyes, he is able to discuss age-old religious concepts as if they were new, alive, and kicking in his heart. Maybe that's because Brinkmann lives out his days like he says we should, with a deep dependency on God. "When my friends and I got laid off at another production company, we started our own. Now we create spots for universities, retailers, TV shows, but we don't have steady work and can barely clear our bills."

So, what does he do? Nothing. Nothing except enjoy God. Nothing except continue in what he has passion for. And since Brinkmann works behind the scenes as a drummer and a producer, sometimes, he admits, it feels like he's in a cocoon, not directly influencing anyone. Then he's reminded it's his actions, not his words, that speak into people's lives. "I was drumming at this conference and I spent time with a kid who also played the drums. At one point, I got off stage and told him, 'Your turn, you play in the band tonight.'

"Later his dad said to me, 'You have no idea the impact you made on my son!' And I said, 'You're right. I don't.' I just wanted him to enjoy life and worship. But that interaction will probably go farther than I know."

Brinkmann has been drumming in Jason Upton's band for the past few years at events like The Call, a twelve-hour day of fasting, praying, and repentance in open venues across the nation. At both The Call D.C. and The Call New England, Brinkmann was overwhelmed by how radically the people there were able to approach God.

"When I was younger, church leaders had to lure kids to youth group with pizza and roller skates. But now, these people—teenagers, college students—were just showing up in hoards. They weren't asking for help with their math test, either. They were in tears, praying for their friends who were on drugs. They were openly pleading with God, exposed like I'd never seen."

Being exposed is a tricky thing in our performance-based and image-driven culture. But in his work, music, and life, Brinkmann continually aims to be exposed: open and intimate with God, knowing that is essentially all He wants us to be.—*Jennifer Ashley*

I.AM.RELEVANT

JULIANA ROSIC

AGE:25
BIRTHPLACE:VENTURA, CALIFORNIA
OCCUPATION:WRITER, MISSIONARY

Reckless, irresponsible, even rebellious. That's what faith feels like for Juliana Rosic. "I'm very non-commital and always looking for something new and exciting. But, Jesus isn't a religion that I'm tied down to. He's a person—the ultimate adventurer, really, and getting to know Him is totally incredible."

When she reads the first few books of the New Testament, Rosic finds that Jesus is a lot like people in our generation—completely against the status quo. "He had a career, but it wasn't a desk job. He traveled, didn't do what was expected of him, and risked everything to help people from all walks of life."

And that's what keeps Rosic going—she's traveled to Guatamala, Nicauraga, Croatia, and China in order to get to know people and tell them just how incredible it is to discover God. "I have a theory about people who do this kind of work," she says. "I think all missionaries in their genetic make-up have a strain of the crazy in them."

Call it crazy, call it faithful and bold—Rosic spent two years in a country she never dreamed she'd end up in. "I don't even like Chinese food!" she laughs. "But, when the job opened up in China, I heard the words go forward—in books I was reading, music I was listening to, and especially while I was praying. I knew from the story of Jesus walking on water that the only way Peter was able to get closer to Jesus was to get out of the boat and go forward."

And living and working in China required her to take risks like never before. Within China's communist (and therefore atheist) government, residents must inform the government if they believe in God. They can't plan public gatherings like Bible studies without notifying the higher-ups. And forget about talking about faith in email or over the phone—the government keeps a close watch over all forms of communication too.

So, Rosic created a code to communicate with American friends over the Internet. She also had to use covert phrases with Chinese friends to invite them to underground Bible discussions held at her apartment. "Most people meet secretly in people's homes for a smaller form of church. That way they can legally meet without the government knowing," Rosic explains.

And although she sometimes feels like she's missing out on a lot of the attractive benefits American life can offer—the stability of a job, house, and family—Rosic continues to go forward, convinced God is providing for her in other amazing ways.

"I may not have a 401K plan or insurance," she says. "I don't even have a car. But ever since I was twelve and working on a housing project in Mexico, I realized that helping people is more fulfilling than anything else. Some people think I'm being irresponsible and not looking out for my future, but I know I'm taken care of—emotionally and spiritually—in ways that aren't recognized by society, but are immeasurable in the long run."
—Jennifer Ashley

KIM DAUGHERTY

AGE:35
BIRTHPLACE:HATTIESBURG, MISSISSIPPI
OCCUPATION:PHILANTHROPIST

When Kim Daugherty and her husband, Robert, began their careers, they prayed God would always help them to be good stewards of whatever resources they had. Her mother, who passed away in 1999, taught her to give back to God by helping others in need. God has answered that prayer.

Kim worked for several years selling software systems for companies like Oracle and Portal Software. With some very good sales years, she found herself in the situation where she had more income than the family needed. By 2000, they had saved a significant amount of money and wanted to use it in a way that would honor God. "We were initially searching for a project to honor my mother's memory," she says, "because my mother had passed away in the year prior to that and so we wanted to do something that would be focused on children and ministering to children."

Her mother took special interest in the needs of underprivileged children in the small

Mississippi town of Petal, where Kim grew up. She taught her own children to concern themselves with the needs of others and to share the blessings that God has given them.

When the couple approached their missions pastor with the desire to give to a project that would provide for children in need, he suggested a church in the Philippines. Its leaders wanted to build a ministry center where they could work with children from several of Manila's impoverished communities. Many of the children had no opportunity for schooling and little hope in life. "We were impressed they had 1,000 people in the congregation, and 300 were volunteers in the children's program," she says. "Even though economically they couldn't afford to build a ministry center, they certainly were putting their time and effort into ministering to the children."

Kim and Robert donated about $70,000 for the ministry center and traveled to Manila last year for its dedication. In the six months since it was completed, the church has grown 60 percent. It is also being used to train those working with children in other parts of the Philippines, as well as in China, Thailand, and India.

Kim recently left her job in sales and invested in rental properties around Georgia. Her new role allows her more time with her family, but she plans on continuing to use her resources to help ministries lay a strong foundation for future charity work. Their latest gift of $15,000 is being used to build a church on the remote Philippine island of Mindoro.

By praying years ago for God's help to use future resources for His glory, the Daughertys have resisted the temptation to use their wealth on a lavish lifestyle and unnecessary luxuries. Kim also credits her mother's influence." "We feel like her life was cut short, but the time that she was here she lived life to the fullest and believed that part of life was giving to others."—*Josh Jackson*

I.AM.RELEVANT

ERIK JOHNSON

AGE:27
BIRTHPLACE:REDDING, CALIFORNIA
OCCUPATION:PEACE CORP VOLUNTEER, ENVIRONMENTAL ENGINEER

What if you sat cramped on an international flight for more than eight hours, were picked up by officials at the airport, and were tossed in the back of rusty pick-up truck for a two hour ride down a dirt road to arrive at your new home for the next few years: a village of 700 that was just demolished by a category five hurricane, the worst in existence. The church is swept from its foundation; only a wasteland of concrete and weeds remain. The dam is broken. Bridges are washed out. Roofs are stripped off of houses. And the crops: passion fruit, pineapple, and cacao, all destroyed. The people's faith, that's gone too. When you ask your new neighbors how they are doing, you're met with a handful of responses: "I'm living, nothing else." "I'm living until God decides differently," and most commonly, your new neighbors look you straight in the eye and say, "Estoy in la lucha": I am in the battle.

And you have been sent to rebuild the town: not just their water system, but their spirit, their faith in living.

That seemingly impossible mission is what Erik Johnson faced on his first assignment in the Peace Corps, just a few months after graduating from college. "There was no hope at all in the town. And I was just one person," Johnson recalls, only weeks after returning from his two-year stint in the Monte Plata province of the Dominican Republic. "I thought it would be easy to get people to work together, but they had such a dim outlook; no one was ready to make changes."

Soon enough, though, the church was reconstructed. And it became a sign of new hope in the midst of chaos. "Changes had little to do with me," Johnson realizes. "God was orchestrating everything. He was the one convincing the people to roll up their sleeves, give up their siesta, and start rebuilding their lives."

And in a village without many resources, work was laborious. To create a water system that would collect rainwater for everyone, Johnson led the men on forty-five minute hikes to dig trenches through extreme heat and rain until sundown. Women followed up the mountain, carrying thirty-pound cast iron pots and 150 pounds of rice and lentil beans to feed their family as they worked. Townspeople rode for miles on mules to bring in cement.

In the end, Johnson was fortunate enough to witness change. Not only in the land, but in the people. "One week before I was scheduled to leave, we inaugurated the water system with a community-wide celebration. People played guitars, tambourines, accordions. We even had a water fight with the new faucet. Everyone came together to embrace their accomplishments.

"While I was there I would mumble to myself a few times every day: What doesn't kill you makes you stronger, and I think that became true not only for me, but for the people of Frias. Watching their faith restore over time completely strengthened mine."
—*Jennifer Ashley*

NICK TURNBULL

AGE:31
BIRTHPLACE:WANTAGE, OXFORDSHIRE, UK
OCCUPATION:MINISTER

The year 2000: Nick Turnbull was a young minister and youth leader at a successful church in the south of England. He was progressive, tapped into culture, had a loyal constituency of young people who trusted him wholeheartedly … trés cool and together, from any vantage point. His job—running a congregation that does church differently and developing the community work of the church—was a dream come true. The job and the life journey were both about asking, and attempting answers to, the question of how to become an emerging church that can keep all the richness of the past, engage and be relevant in the present and still be around for the future.

Then his three-year-old son, Joshua, was diagnosed with brain cancer. To say that Turnbull's life would never be the same again would be cliché, but true.

Joshua died on July 12, 2001, but in his four years on earth—and many more to be spent in the hearts of those who loved him—Joshua created a span of love and influence that changes the world for those who come in contact with his story. Turnbull says, "No one person has inspired me as much as my little four-year-old son."

For the past six months, Turnbull has been sorting through a barrage of emotions and thoughts that most of us may never gain the experience to understand. Through it all he has used his journal as a place for his most poignant honesty and reflection. He has recently given some thought to allowing this chronicle into the public space:

> Some say life was on pause. I'm not sure. Perhaps life actually stopped and now a new record will start to play. One that sounds different. It may have a different tempo. It could possibly have very different lyrics, telling another story…

> Joshua Aaron Turnbull is now not here with us. He no longer physically lives here in this family, but only in our hearts. He leaves such a void it hurts beyond anything imaginable. No more walks. No more parks. No more football. No more bike rides. And so it ends.

> …You touched more lives in four years than most do in a normal lifetime. But still more to touch. More lives to touch that will never be the same as a result of what your life stood for. This is only the start little man. Your legend will live on. Live on to turn people to Jesus, to change people into being more like him.

As Turnbull journeys on, contemplating his son's life, his own life, his role in others' lives and his role in the church, he realizes his responsibility. "This is no easy task, nor are there any quick-fix answers," he says. "As a leader of a church I can have a voice and influence, not to change things to my personal agenda, but to ask the hard questions that I fear not many are asking." —*Daniel Miller*

HOLLY RANKIN

AGE:29
BIRTHPLACE:BROOKSVILLE, FLORIDA
OCCUPATION:YOUTH TRAINER, ADJUNCT PROFESSOR

Holly Rankin is a young woman with a knack for youth ministry in a world of older men who are all about abstract theology. She is a leader in a liturgical tradition gaining momentum after decades of being out of favor. Most people would see a woman facing upstream. Most people would bail if put in her position. But she's not most people. Rankin is in the perfect place for her, and she is thriving.

Rankin is an adjunct professor at Trinity Episcopal School for Ministry. "These days, at least for the next couple of years, I'm mentoring a group of Rock the World youth ministers/church planters as they walk through seminary," she says. "Like most seminaries, Trinity is a place of great thought and Christian formation, but also a very modern institution. Our students have allowed themselves to question the foundational concepts and ideas that everything is built upon at the school and are thinking through it using different metaphors as they both learn about and do ministry.

"We've questioned the way we've always done youth ministry as well," she says. "Why do we have evangelistic retreats? What is evangelism anyway? These are tough conversations. I, as the professor and mentor, do not have hard and fast answers for these things and am actually continually presenting more questions for the students."

Rankin is currently "trading in" (as she puts it) her Masters in Missions and Evangelism and upgrading to a Master of Divinity so she can be ordained in the Episcopal Church. She's also planning to pursue Ph.D. work—possibly in education, working in epistemology and how development, specifically faith development, is changing in our culture. She says her "hope and dream is to be part of a church planting team that will use the Anglican heritage including symbols and liturgy to give a voice and a statement of worship to people in today's culture."

In a church full of passives, only concerned with what's "new" and "cool," Rankin is actually applying a thinking faith that is tackling the tough issues that face the church today. She has also put herself in a place to help lead the church in the direction it must go if it is to survive this new century.

Change is constantly being formed and fueled by quiet thinkers and doers just like Rankin. She may be swimming against the tide, but odds are good that those of us watching from the shore will soon see that tide turn. —*Daniel Miller*

I.AM.RELEVANT

TOM
OLEWE, M.D.

AGE:32
BIRTHPLACE:KISUMU, KENYA
OCCUPATION:PHYSICIAN

Medical school students are supposed to lead lives of intense study, sealing themselves off from the outside world lest some distraction keep them from their goals of a good private practice, a big house, and time for golf. Somehow, Tom Olewe never got that memo.

In between making rounds and cramming for exams at the University of Nairobi, the Kenya native found time to play soccer and get to know some of the kids in one of the city's many slums. The desperate conditions in which they lived— with rivers of sewage flowing openly, no hope for school, and a vacant lot to call home—made the trappings of a wealthy practice seem irrelevant. He had wanted to work with children long before he dreamed of becoming a doctor, and he was becoming increasingly frustrated with the detached, clinical approach of his teachers and fellow students.

A breaking point came when a patient in the teaching hospital was diagnosed with a rarely seen disease, Cushing Syndrome. The teacher was very excited and one by one, enthusiastic students uncovered the suffering, terrified, and naked woman to view the interesting case. "People were just cases," Olewe says. "I thought there had to be a better way to minister to people than just looking for diseases."

I.AM.RELEVANT

After graduating in 1997, with few resources and virtually no income, Olewe decided to work full-time trying to help improve the living conditions of Nairobi's 60,000 street children. He began VIPs Street Child Ministry, the first medical outreach in Kenya's capital. He targeted the Mathare neighborhood, a notorious slum filled with prostitutes and thieves, all addicted to sniffing cheap glues. But because Olewe spent so much time with some of the most violent teenage boys—caring for their problems and earning their trust—he was soon able to enter this violent world without fear. "It was very unsafe initially when we went," he says, "but the more we visit these people, the more they accept us. We've had occasions where we've had to treat some thugs who were assaulted the previous night. And those end up being our security details. They won't let anyone touch you."

As he looked after their medical needs, he showed these kids—who were treated as outcasts by society—that God loves them and desires a better future for them. The transformation in their lives has been nothing short of a miracle. About twenty-five older teenage boys are now living examples of the power of Christ. And the change in their lives has made life better for everyone in their little corner of Mathare because the older boys were the biggest source of crime—raping girls and younger boys, paying for prostitutes, and stealing from older residents.

The burden on Olewe's heart remains heavy for those that have not yet been reached, but seeing the transforming power of God's love shed light in this dark world keeps him energized to bring healing and hope to the street children of Nairobi.—*Josh Jackson*

MAREK KRAJCI

AGE:27
BIRTHPLACE:BRATISLAVA, SLOVAKIA
OCCUPATION:PEDIATRICIAN

Marek Krajci wakes up at 6 A.M. and rubs the sleep out of his eyes. Every week is a game of sleep deprivation—losing sleep all week and then, hopefully, making it back on the weekend. When he walks out of his apartment in Petrzalka, a neighborhood in Bratislava, Slovakia, he is faced with the sight of hundreds of apartment buildings identical to his: huge concrete blocks with no distinguishing characteristics whatsoever—from an airplane it probably looks like a giant cemetery. This vast collection of headstones houses a total of 130,000 people. Krajci lives on the far west side. From the roof of his building strong arms could toss rocks into Austria. During communism, however, even the stones were not permitted to cross.

Krajci gratefully climbs into his newly-acquired-but-definitely-not-new car. Driving to work means he saves himself an extra hour not having to take the crowded and poorly scheduled public transportation. He makes his way to the Children's University Hospital where he begins his day in the department of Children's Cardio Surgery as a pediatrician.

During communism, in order to get into medical school, one was required to be "clean." Status positions under communism required party allegiance and no associations with any subversive groups. Krajci would never be "clean" because his family was Christian. Fortunately, the Communist regime fell before he started to think about medicine.

The hospital where Krajci works is the only clean—literally, this time—children's hospital in Slovakia. In spite of the bad economical situation in Slovakia and an inadequate federal system for financing medicine, Krajci's department is fairly well equipped, because their financing comes from sponsors. The department head is an excellent specialist, and under his direction, theirs is among the best children's cardio surgical centers in the world. They operate not only on Slovak children, but on children from all over Europe. They are, as far as health care goes, a small oasis. Everything else around them is much worse. It is only thanks to the clout of the head surgeon and their excellent results that they are able to achieve such success.

When he does get time away from work, Krajci plays keys in a Christian band which performs throughout the city. The concerts are intended to bring a sense of unity and hope to a confused and downtrodden society. He often has practices during the week on top of an already busy schedule of Christian events all over Bratislava. The old Ford is even more of a godsend when it comes time to get home after a late planning meeting across town.

Tonight, however, is not one of those nights. In the couple of hours he has after work, he manages to speak with his fiancée, Kamila, on the mobile phone and take care of normal everyday business around the apartment. He has some time to read a few pages and scribble some notes—prayers, lyrics, work—before crashing hard in his bed.

What's that noise? Oh, it's 6 A.M. again. —*Daniel Miller*

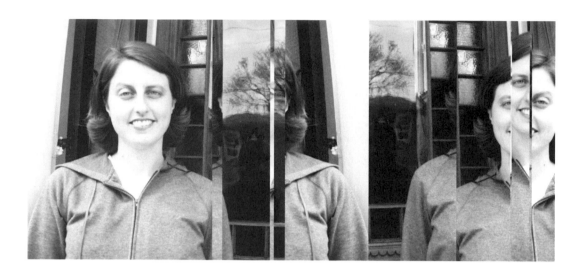

STEPHANIE KRUG

AGE:28
BIRTHPLACE:JACKSONVILLE, FLORIDA
OCCUPATION:SOCIAL WORKER

Growing up in Ft. Valley—a small town outside of Macon, Georgia—Stephanie Krug didn't think much about the racial tension around her. The town was divided black and white along the railroad tracks, and even into the 1990s, the high school held separate proms for the black and white students.

While she was in college at the University of Georgia, two summer experiences in opposite hemispheres opened her eyes to the problems of racial injustice. "When I went to Africa and the next summer did a Meals On Wheels program in the poorer communities of Athens [Georgia], I saw the same kind of poverty in the states that I'd seen overseas in a third world country. And that gave me a great desire to serve the poor here in the states."

Krug now lives in an impoverished all-black community in New Orleans, working with Desire Street Ministries, helping develop leaders within the community to bring real change to their neighborhoods. Always behind the scenes, she organizes Bible studies, provides assistance to families in need, and helps unite pastors in the community. One of her latest projects has been to help develop the Urban Institute of Theology, giving local pastors the chance to get a seminary education without leaving the needs of the community.

"I'm not the type of person who wants to be up front," she says. "It's cool for me to be able to type something or help call and invite people for [the Sunday school teacher] Dionne, who's from the community, knows the kids, and is a dynamic teacher. I think it's a real significant role to play to be able to serve."

Living in such an urban setting has not been without its challenges. On New Year's Eve she woke up to machine gun fire in place of firecrackers. Gang violence has taken the lives of many of the neighborhood's young men, including one of her co-workers in the summer of 2001. He was the brother of Krug's pastor—the third brother he's lost to gang violence. "It's so hard for me, but people in our community deal with that on a regular basis. I went to work today, and someone had been shot last night. It's just a reality here that people are always losing their family members to violence or have lost family members to drugs. In some ways you become callous, and other ways you're continually hurting for those around you. It's not just something you see on TV, but it's the women in your Bible studies' brother or sister."

Still, Krug loves her new community and has more trouble now adapting to her old culture when she goes home. She recently bought a house in the neighborhood and has no intentions of leaving any time soon. "People say, 'It's such a sacrifice that you would live in such a terrible neighborhood and give up so many things,' and I really can't quite figure out what I've given up. I don't think I've given up much."—*Josh Jackson*

I.AM.RELEVANT

REBECCA HEIDGERD

AGE:31
BIRTHPLACE:FORT LAUDERDALE, FLORIDA
OCCUPATION:COMMUNICATIONS COORDINATOR

Because she is already an accomplished writer, traveler, activist, and thinker, writing about Rebecca Heidgerd should be done with healthy amounts of humility and fear. Fortunately, she is already working on her memoirs, so perhaps she can best articulate her own story:

> I remember being fairly young and knowing that I wanted to help people with my life, to make their life better. I knew that money would never be that important to me; although it seemed appealing at times, I would never equate it with happiness or success. I also knew that I didn't want to stay in South Florida for the rest of my life; I wanted to learn firsthand about the cultures of other people and nations, and

never take what I had in America for granted.

Throw in a few quite full years—a missions trip to the projects of New Orleans, graduation from Gordon College in Boston, a summer in Nairobi as a Communications Intern for Wycliffe Bible Translators, hiking the Adirondack Mountains and traveling to Aruba, Bonaire, Andalusia, the Canary Islands, Israel, the Virgin Islands, the Bahamas, and Bermuda while working as a travel writer for *Recommend Magazine*—and then came the decision to move into a career that was not only a career, but a meaningful journey as well. Rebecca went back to Boston to begin with ALS-Therapy Development Foundation:

> On the spot, I knew it was a place I could embrace the day to day. I would be corresponding with patients, their families and friends, and responsible for getting information to them about their disease and what the Foundation was doing. As a nonprofit biotech, ALS-TDF was pursuing therapies that could cure ALS—a job for-profit biotechs would never undertake because the market (the 30,000 ALS patients that die in an average of two to five years) is not considered large enough for it to be profitable.

> Sometimes I fear that after this job, I will only be disappointed. The reason I fear not enjoying anywhere else? [Because] I know I am tangibly helping people. I receive it in emails nearly daily. "Thank you for giving us hope … my son was diagnosed with ALS two months ago. He has a wife and two kids under the age of six." "You are the only place that gives me the information I need." "Thank you so much for the work you do!"

Heidgerd says she wishes the church was as dedicated to meeting the needs of the sick and dying as her organization is. "I see who Christ was more in my 'secular' workplace than I do in the churches I have walked into," she says. "And I often wonder what would happen if the church was as open to new solutions and as committed to helping those alive today as my workplace is." Heidgerd's desire is to be a part of those solutions. —*Daniel Miller*

CHRIS SEAY

AGE:30
BIRTHPLACE:HOUSTON, TEXAS
OCCUPATION:PASTOR

Chris Seay has always known how to draw a crowd. It started at his suburban Houston high school, where the Bible study he started with "a couple of" Christians in the space of a few weeks drew 100-plus crowds. Next he started throwing parties, alternatives to standard high school drunkfests, and drew 300-500 people. "Everybody just wanted to be part of something," Seay says. "I learned if I could articulate something worth being part of, a faith that was really exciting, people would be part of it."

It was an early lesson in responding to situations that challenged his faith: "There were no strong spiritual influences" at the school, he says. "I figured, either I'm going to do the rebellious thing, or I'm going to find my gifts."

Seay has kept building on those gifts. He was a freshly ordained pastor when, lying in a Waco hospital with appendicitis, he perceived God's call to start a church on January

15—six weeks away. So Seay started University Baptist Church for $6,000—"on my Amex card, because it was the only one that didn't have a limit," he says. The first Sunday, 280 congregants worshiped at UBC, and within six weeks, the number was 600. Seay was twenty-two years old.

UBC appealed to many previously unchurched and unbelieving postmoderns, as does Seay's current church, Ecclesia. A Houston congregation serving an eclectic, artsy, and heavily gay urban neighborhood, Ecclesisa just opened the Taft building, an art gallery, performance space, café, bookstore, and community house.

Chief among Seay's gifts is translating the Gospel of Christ into a language comprehensible to his young, culturally sophisticated audience. Seay takes the charge seriously, and it's the reason he eschews traditional paths such as seminary education. "Culture is changing pretty rapidly, totally reinventing itself every two and a half years," he says, citing research by the Pepsi Corporation. "Given that context, to spend any time trying to figure out [ministry] practice in the abstract is a waste of time.

"Seminaries teach more in terms of practice and less in terms of basic, missional theology," Seay says. "Often you have missions departments that are separate from theology departments, and each is completely ineffective without the other." Seay aims to integrate practical experience, theological training, and cultural engagement with his upcoming project, a Christian leadership development program that could be an alternative to seminary for some. Instead of receiving grades, participants will develop a portfolio demonstrating accomplishments in various areas of ministry.

Seay hopes a new generation of church leaders will find new ways to communicate historic Christian faith to a culture steeped in postmodernism. "The modern church said that faith was based on accepting factual propositions. If you don't have fact, you don't have anything. The scariest part of the postmodern context is that you throw out reason, doctrine, and totally base faith on experience. That scares the hell out of me. But there's a healthy part right in the middle. That's where I hope you land."—*Jenny S. Johnson*

I.AM.RELEVANT

ABOUT THE AUTHORS

Jennifer Ashley, 27, is a fiction writer, poet, and freelancer who holds a master's in English with an emphasis in creative writing. She and her husband Charles attend Trinity Presbyterian Church in San Luis Obispo, California.

John M. De Marco, 34, is a freelance and fiction writer and a United Methodist pastor based in West Palm Beach, Florida. A former newspaper reporter and magazine editor, De Marco has written for numerous magazines, websites, and companies across a variety of industries.

Margaret Feinberg, 27, is a writer based in Steamboat Springs, Colorado. She has written for a variety of nationally recognized magazines and is a contributing writer to both *Enjoying God: Embracing Intimacy with the Heavenly Father and I Am Relevant*. Her most recent work is *God Whispers: Learning to Hear His Voice*. When she is not writing, she can be found enjoying the outdoors of Colorado hiking, snowshoeing, or working as a ski instructor.

Josh Jackson, 30, is editor of *Paste Magazine*, a quarterly publication covering signs of life in music and culture, and PasteMusic.com, an online retail site devoted to independent artists whose music connects to the soul. He lives in Decatur, Georgia, with his wife, Lori, and two daughters.

Jenny Staff Johnson, 31, writes about faith and culture from her home in Houston, Texas. She and her husband run Strange Land Books, a non-profit bookstore specializing in literature, culture studies, and Christian theology.

Bobby Kim, 22, is a writer/photographer for *Stance*, *Giant Robot*, *JapanZine*, *Lotus*, *Evil Monito*, *Asian Diversity*, *KoreAm*, and of course, *RELEVANTmagazine.com*. In his spare time, he digs on post-pop graffiti-influenced art, music, toys, youth subculture, fashion, apologetics, and of course, Jesus Christ. This fall, he will start his treacherous journey through law school. Of course!

Daniel Miller, 27, is a musician, writer, technologist, photographer, digital artist, and social advocate. He was born and raised in Pennsylvania, earned his B.S. degree in psychology from the University of Arizona, and now resides in Florida. He is married to Miriam, a Slovak native, and they travel frequently to Europe.

PHOTO CREDITS

ALSO FROM RELEVANT BOOKS

THE GOSPEL ACCORDING TO TONY SOPRANO

THE GOSPEL ACCORDING TO TONY SOPRANO reveals that *The Sopranos* is much like a biblical parable. It provokes us, challenges us, and pries back the exterior to peek into the darkest parts of our souls. This book explores the many reasons why the show has connected so deeply with American culture and exposes the mysteries of life and faith that emerges just behind the curtains of baked ziti and Armani suits.

RESTLESS PILGRIM: The Spiritual Journey Of Bob Dylan

A curious icon of popular culture, yet distinct in his Judeo-Christian expressions, Bob Dylan doesn't fit neatly into the typical rock 'n' roll mold. RESTLESS PILGRIM wrestles with the seemingly contradictory facts of Dylan's preoccupation with Jesus and his own Jewish heritage, by looking through the lens of this reluctant legend's four-decade career.

GOD WHISPERS: Learning To Hear His Voice

We have questions. God has answers. We just don't always hear them. GOD WHISPERS challenges readers to live with a tender heart as well as open eyes and ears to the countless ways in which God speaks.

IF YOU LIKE THIS BOOK, YOU'LL LOVE
RELEVANTMAGAZINE.COM

RELEVANTMAGAZINE.COM is an out-of-the-box publication covering God, life and progressive culture like nothing else. Updated with new content daily, the site discusses faith, career, relationships, music and more from an intelligent, God-centered perspective. In style, substance and focus, there's nothing like RELEVANTMAGAZINE.COM.

FEATURING:
[-] Articles, columns, news and reviews updated daily
[-] Message boards and chat
[-] Weekly newsletter
[-] Free downloads
[-] Online store with a ton of RELEVANT gear and books

[-] Want to be updated on hot new features and news from RELEVANT? Sign up for our weekly email, 850 WORDS OF RELEVANT. It's the best email you'll receive all week.